CW01021268

Genius in 9 Symphonies

Genius in 9 Symphonies

How Beethoven Reinvented Music

With a forward by Edward Dickinson,

Professor emeritus of the History of Music,

Oberlin College

Jerome Bengis

Rose Mason Press

Douglassville, PA USA

Genius in 9 Symphonies: How Beethoven Reinvented Music.
Copyright © 2021 by Susanna Lee.
All rights reserved.
--
Beethoven and His Nine Symphonies by Jerome Bengis.
Forward by Edward Dickinson.
Preface by Michael Bengis.
Introduction by Susanna Lee.
About the Author by Michael Bengis.
About the Cover by Michael Bengis.
Afterword by Susanna Lee.

Edited by Susanna Lee.
Cover, layout, and design by Susanna Lee.

Summary: Close analysis of the symphonic works of Beethoven.

Subjects: Beethoven; Beethoven -- Symphonies; Composers -- Beethoven; Music appreciation -- Beethoven.

Tags: Beethoven, Beethoven's symphonies, Music appreciation, Music history.

Table of Contents: A Few Words by the Author -- Forward -- Preface -- Introduction -- Before Beethoven -- He Is Born -- The Symphony No. 1 in C major, Opus 21 -- The Symphony No. 2 in D major, Opus 36 -- The Third Symphony in E Flat, Opus 55 -- The Fourth Symphony in B Flat, Opus 60 -- The Fifth Symphony in C minor, Opus 67 -- The Sixth Symphony in F, Opus 68 -- The Seventh Symphony in A major, Opus 92 -- The Eighth Symphony in F major, Opus 93 -- The Ninth Symphony in D minor, Opus 125 -- A Final Consideration of Beethoven and His Achievements -- Notes -- About the Author -- Afterword -- About the Cover.

First edition.

Published by Rose Mason Press.

Dedication

To those who bring children to hear the symphony orchestra

"Teach us how to love each other,
Lift us to the Joy Divine."

~ Henry van Dyke, 1907

CONTENTS

A Few Words by the Author   *ii*

Forward by Edward Dickinson   *iii*

Preface by Michael Bengis   *iv*

Introduction by Susanna Lee   *vii*

Beethoven and His Nine Symphonies

    Before Beethoven   2

    He Is Born   4

    The Symphony No. 1 in C major, Opus 21   6

    The Symphony No. 2 in D major, Opus 36   9

    The Third Symphony in E Flat, Opus 55   13

    The Fourth Symphony in B Flat, Opus 60   26

    The Fifth Symphony in C minor, Opus 67   30

    The Sixth Symphony in F, Opus 68   36

    The Seventh Symphony in A major, Opus 92   44

    The Eighth Symphony in F major, Opus 93   50

    The Ninth Symphony in D minor, Opus 125   53

    A Final Consideration of Beethoven and His

       Achievements   61

    Notes   63

Afterword by Susanna Lee   *64*

About the Author by Michael Bengis   *66*

About the Cover by Michael Bengis   *67*

A FEW WORDS BY THE AUTHOR

This booklet is intended as a little journey into the realms of Beethoven's symphonic music. It is not a technical note book: it is a record of personal joys derived from listening to music. All analysis contained herein was inspired by a love of music, not by a duty toward it: it is only by loving music that we can grow to understand it. And once it is understood, it is no longer a stranger which comes to visit us from time to time, but a friend—a confessor as well as a physician. To bring the casual music lovers into closer communion with this great confessor and physician,—that is the purpose to which this booklet is dedicated.

The "casual music lover"—to use the phrase which has already been mentioned—constitutes the majority of the average musical audience. The professional musicians, as well as the musical amateurs, are greatly in the minority: music is something which all may listen to, but which few may understand. Yet it seems that every book dealing with some phase of music is written only for the musician. In writing this booklet, I have therefore remembered the vast majority of music lovers who know little or nothing of music technically. While I have found it quite impossible to altogether omit all musical terms, I have endeavored to omit them wherever possible, or to replace them with more understandable language.

The comments on the dangers of word pictures to describe programme music may seem inconsistent with my own descriptive tendencies. For this I offer no apology, but repeat what I say elsewhere: that these fragmentary descriptions are mentioned only to convey to the reader some of those many images which music brings to my own mind. They are, in short, intended only as personal impressions, for music must evoke some picture in any mind that is even slightly imaginative. For anyone to suppose that I intend him to imagine what I do, is for him to lose rather than to gain by my impressions.

Jerome Bengis

New York

October, 1937

FORWARD

It gives me pleasure to commend this monograph on the symphonies of Beethoven, by Mr. Bengis, to all, musicians or laymen, who have already felt the power and beauty of these incomparable creations. A great deal has already been written about Beethoven's works, but they will always call for new interpretation, as do all products of supreme genius. For such works not only express emotions—they also reflect emotion that is brought to them and thereby made further to realize itself.

Most of the previous expositions of Beethoven's symphonies consist of technical analysis of form and structure. These have their value—they are in fact indispensable. But they only open the way to a comprehension of the composer's purpose and its significance. It is a recognition of this supreme motive and achievement that Mr. Bengis has striven to present, and he has done this in the only way possible, viz. by describing his own intellectual and spiritual responses. He has accomplished his task with an insight and with a literary skill that are worthy of admiration.

His task was difficult in its very nature, but he has avoided the peril that is most immanent in such a task, which I am glad that in his discussion of certain movements of the symphonies I should be inclined to temper his enthusiasm and in other movements to increase it. That is to say, that his appreciations are not conventional, but highly personal and spontaneous. This gives them conviction as well as charm. The close of his monograph is an exquisite piece of literary art. It throws back upon his whole meditation a tender light as of gratitude to the master for his great gift to humanity.

Edward Dickinson
Professor emeritus of the History of Music
Oberlin College

PREFACE

My uncle Jerome was the youngest of six children. His parents arrived here from Vilna (then Poland) Russia in 1905. He was a New Yorker by birth, and except for his last few months, lived his entire life in New York City.

I am not sure that Jerome ever completed high school, but he loved to read, and started writing plays at an early age. In his milieu, pre-TV, and even pre-radio, it was not uncommon for families to entertain themselves with music, singing, and the spoken word. Thus, there were many readings of plays, with brothers and sisters passing a script around. I'm in my eighties now, but I remember participating in one of these play readings more than seventy years ago. I also remember being chastised for chewing gum while reading my lines.

As to Jerome's experience with the human condition, my uncle once told me that his knowledge on that subject came from his reading and rereading of Ibsen's plays. The play Hedda Gabler was his favorite. I wasn't the only one who felt that Jerome was of an earlier century. A self-educated man without credentials, he made music, art and literature his thing and what he most liked to talk about. Jerome did not play any musical instrument, but he seemed to know, more than most of us, about the workings of an orchestra, and the range and limits of the many instruments.

I remember to this day the enthusiasm he displayed as he described in rapturous tones the delight that awaited me when I would play the 33-rpm record of Beethoven's 6th symphony he then handed me. I can still hear the excitement in his voice as he described the arrival, build up, and eventual fury of the Pastoral Symphony's storm sequence.

As an adult, my uncle earned his living typing (two fingers only) forms and such for the NY State Insurance Fund. His real life began after 5:00 pm each day, when he returned to his Bronx apartment and sat down at his own Remington typewriter. The subjects included Beethoven, of course, but also Mozart and Brahms. These were followed by an imaginative sequel to Crime and Punishment, and he even wrote of Jesus Christ.

As far as I know, only one of Jerome's plays was ever staged, and that happened when Converse College in Spartanburg, South Carolina mounted a production of "The Silent Years." The play presented a depiction of Jesus before the age of thirty, a time when he "increased in wisdom and stature and in favour with God and man." The gospels say no more than this, but Jerome's prose fleshes out the details with what has been called "poetic beauty." The play received commendation from the National Theater Conference in 1944. Jerome did travel to South Carolina to see the weekend performances. It was the biggest thing to hit the town of Spartanburg that weekend of December 10–11, 1949. For those two days at least, Jerome got a taste of what fame might be like. It was the farthest he had ever ventured from NYC. Though he wrote of events far and wide, I think that, for him, New York City held all he needed.

My uncle loved to see a Broadway play, and prices were cheap for the times. As a teenager in the 1950s, I remember one could purchase a seat in the balcony for $2.20, the mezzanine for $3.30, and the orchestra, $4.40. I imagine in the '30s and '40s they were cheaper yet. However, if you grew up in a family of eight, with but one working-class salary, there was not often any "extra" money. Jerome saw many Broadway plays, most of them from the second act on, having walked in with the crowd after the first act intermission and scurrying to an unsold seat.

He'd often write to famous actors of the day, and was more than once invited to a backstage dressing room, post-performance. Offered a martini by a Broadway leading lady at one such impromptu event, he gulped it down, only then to have to leap for the door, in desperate straits—an olive lodged in his throat. Other overtures were more successful, however, and he eventually got to know and establish friendships with the likes of Catherine Cornell and the character actor Joseph Wiseman.

But concert music held for him the ultimate charm. Beyond the nine symphonies, he had fondness for Beethoven's "Triple Concerto" and Hummel's violin concerto. For him, classical music ended as the 19th century ended. He did allow that Samuel Barber's Adagio for Strings was a worthy exception to that rule.

Isabel, Jerome's wife, died in 1994. In less than a year, his own decline began. Because his marriage was childless, my wife and I secured for Jerome a nursing home in Sussex County, NJ. He accepted this last stage of his life in good spirits, but it was downhill from there, and my uncle died in July, 1995.

Michael Bengis

INTRODUCTION

Of all the treasures found while preparing for the estate sale of a long-dead relative, few are more exciting than the discovery of an unpublished literary manuscript of extraordinary value. This treatise on the life and genius of Beethoven provides an in-depth analysis of the joyride experienced by one of Beethoven's faithful listeners, Michael Bengis's uncle Jerome, whose writings were discovered in an attic during the housecleaning preparations preceding the sale of his long-vacant house.

In his youth, decades before the modern distractions of the internet and social media, Jerome Bengis attended performances of the symphony orchestra and recorded his experiences in gorgeous and emotional prose. He wrote with genuine fervor about how Beethoven's nine greatest works touched him, unleashed his own imagination, and allowed him to delve into the mind of the composer. His analysis of the symphonic works, movement by movement, included the timeline of historical events which influenced Beethoven, who expressed in his music both an unwavering optimism and a pure love of all mankind.

Jerome worked days in an office in the Bronx, NY typing insurance forms, but he spent every free minute indulging in the arts, attending the theatre and concerts, and expressing his delight in detailed prose. In "Beethoven and His Nine Symphonies," Jerome pours his heart out, describing his passionate love of Beethoven. On hearing the masterpieces, Jerome's spirit is emancipated. The thrill is as exciting as a rollercoaster ride. So taken is he by Beethoven's genius, Jerome is moved to share his discovery: he writes, painstakingly typing up an eighty-page thesis. He tries to answer for himself his own questions and describe what it is, exactly, that makes Beethoven unique among composers. How is it that Beethoven can make each note shine, and more brilliantly than the note just before?

Jerome describes Beethoven's creative process, not from the viewpoint of an academic or one trained in music criticism, but as an avid and attentive listener who has been swept away in awe on recognizing that Beethoven was developing, with each succeeding symphony, an entirely new way of approaching musical construction. Beethoven was not content to have mastered the entirety of music history and perfected his own technical brilliance—he allowed himself to be influenced by the geniuses of his era and the onward rush of civilization as it was unfolding. He continually strove to invent new ways to express the sea changes humanity was experiencing and to promote understanding of what it means to be human.

Jerome puts Beethoven into historical context, showing how the composer incorporated into his work the social changes roiling throughout the entire world. The composer saw the influence of the charisma and destructive power of Napoleon, the foment of the American and French Revolutions, and the manifestation of the ideas of liberty and the rights of man. His music evokes this new-found independence from both monarchy and from tradition. Beethoven brought the Romantic Age into fruition.

In exploring the evolution of Beethoven's work, Jerome has uncovered evidence of entirely new ways of thinking. Beethoven's Ninth, with its choral masterpiece "Ode to Joy," is an expression of the fullness of human consciousness. It culminates in the rise of the common man with his hopes for a realization of the ideal.

As Edward Dickinson of Oberlin College puts it in his Forward, Jerome's writing is unconventional and enthusiastic. For the modern reader, it is a fresh look at Beethoven through eyes brimming with tears of joy.

If nothing else, these words will give you the language you may have been searching for in order to properly introduce a young child to the mysteries of great music.

Susanna Lee, poet, author of
Sunrise Mountain

Genius in 9 Symphonies

BEETHOVEN

AND

HIS NINE SYMPHONIES

BEFORE BEETHOVEN

Beethoven was born at a period when the times were most ripe for his genius. That was his greatest advantage over Bach. His coming was like that of Prometheus: he brought fire to music, but his predecessors had taught him how not to burn his fingers. They had left a finished torch behind, but Beethoven was to give it fire and set the world aflame. The later romanticists came and poured oil on the fire, but the flames are still essentially Beethoven's.

In the seventeenth century, instrumental music was but a slight means of conveying emotions to the ear. The term "symphony" was at first used like "concerto." A symphony was usually nothing more than an instrumental accompaniment for vocal music, or an instrumental interlude between pauses in singing. Suites and concertos, which were the forerunners of the modern symphony, were soon invented, and Torelli was already bringing the concerto form of the sonata into existence. Soon Bach came with his suites and concertos of contrasting movements, and then Handel followed with his concerti grossi. Christian Bach, who absorbed the Italian style, soon came to London and brought out his clavier sonatas; while Philip Emmanuel Bach, the son of the great father, was already approaching the symphony. It was left for Haydn and Mozart, however, to shape the symphony into its highest form before passing it on into the hands of Beethoven. Haydn was about twenty-seven when he composed his first symphony, and a stream of others followed with amazing spontaneity.

However, the symphony in Haydn's early days was still a matter of little importance. What was Haydn's first symphony, but "a little work in three movements, for two violins, viola, bass, two oboes, and two horns." Gradually the number of instruments were increased: the depth of emotional utterance became more evident; and the symphony became a more finished work of art, gradually terminating in the glorious masterworks of Mozart. With the appearance of the new master, who had fully absorbed his great contemporary's methods, the more personal element was gradually to appear. At first the symphony was of no more importance to Mozart than it had been to Haydn. His first symphony was written at the age of eight, and it was a slight affair. As he matured, however, the promise of the great symphonist slowly appeared. The Symphony in G minor, which was the second of his last symphonic trilogy, contains a stamp of personal character hitherto unrealized even in Haydn's greatest symphonies. His last in C, called the "Jupiter," was the highest and most finished point to which Mozart could soar before leaving the musical heavens ready for Beethoven. He had, however, soared within his own regions of classicism, for Mozart in his most rebellious mood was still a divine classicist. He had not overstepped his own boundaries; the eighteenth century spirit of grace and elegance is predominant even in his last great symphony, but it is tempered with a profound depth of godlike utterance which has well earned for it the title, "Jupiter." The death of Mozart, therefore, which occurred only nine years before the end of the eighteenth century, was like a sublime reminder of the dawning of the new era. For the greatest was yet to come.

HE IS BORN

Beethoven was born only thirty years before the close of the nineteenth century, and, singularly enough, only one year after the birth of that other great conqueror, Napoleon. When he was thirteen years of age, the American Revolution was already at an end, and the spirit of independence was beginning to show itself in Europe. Nineteen years later the French Revolution began, and the voice of human equality sounded far and wide while heads fell to the accompaniment of the monotonous counting of the members of the knitting circle in La Place de la Revolution. There was a change in living, thought, and art. The transformation was as tumultuous and breath-taking as the scherzo of Beethoven's "Eroica." This was another stroke of good fortune for the genius of our musical Prometheus. Not only had the path been cleared for him by his predecessors, but the new spirit of liberation at the close of the eighteenth century definitely voiced Europe's timeliness for its reception of new emancipators. Art was no longer created to please the delicate taste of royal patrons, who hitherto had been the sole supporters of the artist; but the public was regarded as one complete whole, and art consequently took on a more universal aspect. Whereas formerly the artist was concerned chiefly with abstract ideas of classic beauty, he now began to consider the thoughts of the individual in relation to the masses. After Napoleon's downfall, a strong national spirit arose in Germany. The attention of both poet and musician was now focused on German peasant life, and later on German mythology and folk-lore. Years later the German opera was to reach its highest peak of triumphant nationalism in Weber's "Der Freischütz." So began the romantic school of music, of which Beethoven was the founder; and, while the spirit of classicism did not disappear at once, it was at first a guiding light into the new regions of romanticism. Just as Beethoven enters the finale of his "Fifth Symphony" on the bridge leading from the preceding movement, so does he enter his new realm on the bridge of the old, while from beyond the surging waters roar in protest. But Beethoven crosses safely; and Schubert, Weber, Brahms, Schumann, Wagner,

Liszt, Chopin, and all his other musical brethren follow. He is the prophet leading the children of music out of the wilderness and into the light. He is the musical Moses, and in his hand he carries his wand which is to create hitherto unheard-of wonders for men to marvel at.

THE SYMPHONY NO. 1 IN C MAJOR, OPUS 21

B eethoven waited until he was almost thirty years of age before he wrote the first symphony of his immortal nine. Like Brahms he approached the symphonic field with great caution; but, once possessed of the fire of inspiration, he proceeded more rapidly. This was one of the products of his first period, which consisted firstly of his power of imitation, secondly of his power of experimentation, and thirdly of his embryonic powers of originality.

The "First Symphony" is generally regarded as a mere imitation of Mozart and Haydn. Most emphatically this is not so. Many critics of great technical ability have failed to see this merely because they are critics of technique, not of soul-quality. Their technical knowledge does not allow the fullest expansion of their purely imaginative powers of contemplation. Very rarely do they surrender themselves wholly to the spiritual utterances of a symphony; and they end by seeing originality only where technical wonders occur. Proof of this may be found in the work of a certain technician who once wrote of the "irresistible gaiety" of Mozart's G minor symphony. Even such a thorough critic as Jahn found the "expression of perfect happiness in the charm of euphony" in Mozart's Symphony in E Flat. The poignant longing and melancholy of the Second Movement escaped his attention because he was, before all else, a critic of technique, not of soul quality.

First Movement: Adagio molto; allegro con brio

Although Beethoven's "First Symphony" was written in the key of C major, it begins with the chord of the minor in the 7th of C. During Beethoven's time, the critics were outraged and considered this a daring bit of impudence. Today, however, we know better. The chord is quite tame, and the introduction into the main theme does not excite our wonder. The appearance of the main theme, however, startles us somewhat. Its exposition is orthodox, but there is a rugged element of Beethovenish impetuosity in it that seems quite different from Mozart and Haydn. Already, we feel, there is a hint of something greater to come. Later on, when we listen to the prophetic drum passages, we are assured that our first impression was not wrong. Beethoven is beginning to stir; as yet he stirs only a single limb, but soon the whole man will awake.

Second Movement: Andante cantabile con moto

Prometheus goes to sleep again. This is the only movement in the entire symphony which entirely justifies the rococo label placed on it by critics. The very opening is reminiscent of the first few bars of the Second movement of Mozart's G minor symphony. Later on there is some original drum work, but the inner voice of the creator is absent. The movement abounds in lovely curves and passages of gentle beauty. It is like the youthful Shelley awaking to the fresh beauties of the world.

Third Movement: Minuetto a trio

"If ever I allow my muse to slumber, it is only that she may awaken all the stronger." So said Beethoven; and here he gives us a typical example of his muse's awakening. Here, more than in any other part of the symphony, do we catch our first glimpse of the emancipating forces of Beethoven's genius. The tempo of the rococo minuet is quickened; the flowery grace of Mozart and Haydn disappears; the common dance takes on the wider proportions of the varied movements of life. Individuality is breathed into the minuet, and it becomes a scherzo. But for once in his life Beethoven is cautious. To write a scherzo in place of a minuet is bad enough; but to call it a scherzo would be even worse. So Beethoven silences the critics and calls the movement a minuetto; better than that, he marks it only by its tempo, and calls it tempo de minuetto. It is but one of his little jokes, for Beethoven without his sense of humor is not Beethoven.

The trio again reveals the budding master to us. Let us compare this trio with one of the last by Mozart. The middle section of the minuet of the G minor symphony is, in comparison with this one, like the gentle playfulness of a child as compared with the frolics of a bear. As soon as Beethoven becomes bearish, we know he is Beethoven and no one else. Already we have a faint trace of the

7

amiable drolleries of the "Eighth Symphony." But let us have patience; an even more pleasant surprise is at hand: we now approach the finale.

Finale: Allegro molto e vivace

Here is a specimen of Beethoven's early writing which has always been considered imitative of the rococo style; firstly because it follows the old-time quick movement, and secondly because it is scored only for strings, woodwind, two horns, two trumpets, and two drums. True, it is as far from the wide proportions of the finales of the later symphonies as Mozart's concertos are from Beethoven's own "Emperor." It has no ruggedness or glorious power, no titanic individuality; but it is Beethoven and only Beethoven, and to say that it is purely Haydnesque is a serious error. Here we behold Beethoven poking fun at his polished contemporaries, and he seems to be enjoying himself immensely. It is the spiritual, rather than the technical nature of the work, which reveals his own individual nature. Beethoven laughs. It is not the re-echoing laughter of Rabelais, as in the scherzo of the "Eroica"; Beethoven's wit is only like that of Swift, but it is sound, earthly wit. The introduction into the allegro is one of Beethoven's most pleasant fooleries. It is the opening of the string around his package of surprises. He is like a cat that wiggles its body as it prepares for its abrupt leap after an elusive mouse. He goes bouncing into the allegro with a rollicking humor that is altogether exhilarating. That which follows is as refreshing as a cold shower turned on the naked back. Once Beethoven's joy is unloosed, he bounds hither and thither like a young colt. It is a movement of perfect happiness; a miniature rejoicing of the universe on the prophetic sign of what is yet to come.

THE SYMPHONY NO. 2 IN D MAJOR, OPUS 36

First Movement: Adagio molto; allegro con brio

Never did an artist better grasp his new materials than did Beethoven. This symphony is largely a work of experimentation, in which the voices of Mozart and Haydn are almost completely drowned out by the virile tones of the master of the new era. It does not yet reveal the truest Beethovenish spirit, but it is the fullest prediction of the symphonic glories of the future. It is as great an anticipation of the dawning of a new musical era as Nora's final speech from Ibsen's "Doll's House" is of the new dramatic and cultural epoch.

The introduction to the first movement is in itself a great advancement over the introduction to the opening movement of the "First Symphony." Not only is it broader in outline, but it is already a hint of those wonderful prefatory structures of the "Fourth" and "Seventh" symphonies which were later to enthrall Schumann. "When writing your symphonies, remember Beethoven's introductions, and try to do something like them." Thus was the great romanticist to remark to Beethoven's follower, Brahms. As early as the "Second Symphony," a breathless resemblance to a passage in the "Ninth" occurs. It is toward the very end of this remarkable introduction that we encounter a phrase reminiscent of the magnificent beginning of Beethoven's last symphony, wherein chaos seems to break over our heads. Such a resemblance is to occur again in the first movement of the third concerto in C minor for piano and orchestra. The master is already dreaming his titanic conceptions of the future; soon we shall not be able to catch up with him.

Let us observe the characteristic vigor with which Beethoven enters into his main theme. There is something in this which recalls to one's mind the picture of the young naked titan splashing in bubbling water, as seen by Ries who happened to notice the exhibit one fine summer's afternoon. Everything seems to point to

Beethoven's well-being and exuberance of spirits. Beethoven must indeed have been possessed of a giant will to rise above his sufferings, for it was at this very time that he wrote his melancholy Heiligenstadt Testament, in which he cried out in anguish to the whole universe. "Oh man! when you shall read this, reflect that you have wronged me," he wrote as a concluding lamentation over his deafness; and yet herein—in this very symphony which he composed at this period, he embraces mankind with a joyous fullness of heart. The second theme itself—is it not a beautiful anticipation of those drinking songs which are to occur in the trios of the third movements of the "Third," "Fourth," "Seventh," and "Eighth" symphonies? Who could better feel this than Beethoven,— this love of his fellow men for which he lived and created? Universal brotherhood: that was yet to be the all-embracing message of the choral finale of the "Ninth Symphony." This first movement, then, as well as the entire "Second Symphony," is a wholehearted pledge of Beethoven's noblest optimism.

Second Movement: Larghetto

Here is the serenity of the ideal conception of poetry in nature. Again Beethoven advances over his "First Symphony." The opening theme is reminiscent of Mozart's graver moments, and is developed with caressing patience which fills the heart with joy. Here is music that is full of exquisite beauty; music like those softly shaded lines by Keats which begin by speaking of

Seasons of mists and mellow fruitfulness.

Deliciously rounded curves follow one another in one long stream of glowing romanticism. Mild and fragrant confidences are exchanged among the wood-wind instruments. Already the horn passages foretell Beethoven's magic handling of the horns in the later symphonies. The abruptness of the charming close is later to expand into the sudden flashes of wit which are to end such characteristic passages as the scherzo of the "Fourth Symphony." Here everything is welded into one beautiful whole. This is Beethoven's last moment of symphonic serenity before he mounts to the cragged heights of the "Eroica," there to sit and brood over the sorrows and conflicts of the universe. Soon—all too soon are the subtler aspects of human philosophy to spread their more sombre beauty over the face of the civilized world, and everyone is to look upward with expectant glances of questioning.

Third Movement: Scherzo e trio

The master is slowly coming into his own kingdom. The scherzo of the "First Symphony" was but a slight suggestion of what was to be one of Beethoven's greatest contributions to music; now the hint becomes a definite prediction, and a burst of vigorous action follows. The polished grace of the rococo minuets is already a thing of the past. Instead we have a main theme that begins by hitting us right on the heads; good-natured, healthful fun, with Beethovenish drolleries scattered here and there; impish pranks, like those of a hungry bear at feeding time. Childishly simple is the second theme, which pauses long enough for Beethoven to give it a good vigorous cranking before he takes us bouncing back into the principle subject. This is the second of Beethoven's symphonic bursts of laughter. Rabelais is laughing louder.

Fourth Movement: Allegro molto

To say that this even remotely resembles the finales of Mozart or Haydn is ridiculous folly. Only a giant like Beethoven could have written it. The structure of the finale of the "First Symphony" is broadened; the well-balanced humor becomes rough; the youthful spirit of the energetic revolutionist turns aside from conventional refinement, even as it was later to spurn the Viennese aristocracy. Beethoven is like one drunk with youth and the dawning powers of true greatness. The opening theme is like the savage trampling of a young bull. Beethoven will stop at nothing, and if he does pause for an instant, it is only to go bounding forth with greater vigor. He seems to be thinking of Mozart and chuckling to himself: "Ha! If only he could hear this, his ear drums would burst!" For such excesses of vigor were not for the effeminate masters of pure classicism, with their powdered periwigs. Toward the end he slows up a bit, as though to relax himself somewhat; but he fools us: before we can recover our senses, the coda is over. Whereupon we feel inclined to say: "Now again, Beethoven." But Beethoven is determined to say no more; he stops, and we know that his little comedy is at an end.

The Third Symphony in E Flat, Opus 55 "The Eroica"

Beethoven's attitude toward Napoleon, and its consequences

There are two regrettable things about Beethoven's "Eroica Symphony": the first is Beethoven's own attitude toward it; the second, the programmes that have originated therefrom. We know that Beethoven originally dedicated this symphony to Napoleon Bonaparte, who he at first regarded as Europe's symbol of liberty. In the year of 1804, when Ries brought the news to Beethoven that Napoleon had proclaimed himself emperor, the infuriated master tore the title-page off the score, shouting, as he did so, "Then he too is a tyrant: Now he will elevate himself above the world and trample on people's rights!" Whereupon he stamped on the title page with characteristic fury, and changed the dedication to: "Sinfonia Eroica. Dedicated to the memory of a great man." From all this biographers have concluded the following: Firstly, that Beethoven's love of Napoleon was nourished only by his own democratic principles. Secondly, that after Napoleon's assumption of the French crown, Beethoven no longer continued to regard him as a hero. And lastly, that the symphony itself is concerned only with the life and death of Napoleon.

Let us burst these fictitious bubbles at once. We must begin by examining Beethoven's attitude toward Napoleon somewhat more closely than his romantic biographers are generally accustomed to. Should we re-read Ries's original account of Beethoven's fury on learning of Napoleon's assumption of the crown, we may observe that the master's reaction was not one of mere disappointment, but of intense emotional disturbance. His words, "He will trample on people's rights," was his unconscious means of convincing himself, no less than Ries and Count Lichnowsky, who were then present, that his concern was firstly for the masses, and secondly for himself. But the sad truth is that Beethoven must have felt that here, at last, was one who could command him and exercise a tyrannical power over him. For Beethoven loved power as long as he possessed it, but hated it in anyone else. This truth can have no better illustration than by Beethoven's reaction two years later on hearing of Napoleon's victory over the Prussians in the Battle of Jena. For this monarch of his own domain clenched his fist and said, "If only I knew as much about war as I do about music, I'd conquer him!" Here is the underlying element of Beethoven's attitude toward Napoleon: it was an undercurrent of jealousy, contempt for one who was capable of doing what he himself could accomplish only in music. This is the wondrous—the sublime egotist who illuminated the entire world by his egotism; it is the same giant who not only was pleased with tearing down the musical standards of the past and erecting his own, but who, in spite of his lack of interest in choral writing, exploited even the fields of the opera and the oratorio so that he might feel that he had not left a single field unconquered.

The truth is that few can feel their own insignificance as well as the truly great, for they alone have the inner perceptions necessary for seeing themselves in relation to the world. Poe's outburst, "Not even God is superior to me!", is not so much a revelation of arrogance, as of his wildly intense desire to hide his conscious feeling of insignificance from himself. It is power which the genius seeks,—power in perfection; and the nearer he comes to his distant goal, the further does it seem to move from him. He would be greater and loftier, and have all men pay him homage, but men take little, if any, notice of him while he lives. The great intellect is left to wander alone in the wilderness, and occasionally he gives vent to his emotions by shouting out his supreme knowledge of his superiority to the world. But the very fact that they must shout it out, as Beethoven himself often did, is a sign that he is wont to experience moments of gnawing uncertainty.

Yes, they all too often feel their insignificance, these men who live to be a heritage to history. On the other hand, they are completely aware of their superiority to the common individual. This inner feeling of insignificance, which they feel in spite of their knowledge of their great power, is the one thing they are constantly seeking to outgrow; and they end by overbalancing the scales of common reason. Beethoven knew it was impossible for him to be as great a general as a musician; yet he doted on the thought all the same. He wanted to be a great choral writer as well, and for this he found an outlet mainly in his "Mount of Olives," "Fidelio," the "Missa Solemnis," and the last movement of the "Ninth Symphony." But for the other thing—his envious attitude toward Napoleon,—he could find no outlet in actual means of warfare, so he unconsciously disguised his resentment by pretending that he regarded him as a symbol of tyranny. Yet, some years later, when he has almost convinced himself that Napoleon is no longer his hero, he hears that the emperor is entering Vienna, and that he will probably demand to see that city's most renowned artists; whereupon, with characteristic naiveté, he bends over to a French officer and asks eagerly, "Do you think he will send for *me*?"

Power! power! Beethoven sought power, and power he must have. To his early factotum, Zmeskall, who once lectured to him on morality, he replied, "Devil take you! I want to hear nothing of your moral ideas. Strength is the morality of men who prove themselves superior to others, and it is mine!" If the youthful Beethoven, who had not yet created the "First Symphony" could speak thus, what could be expected of the later man who had already finished the colossal "Third"? Everything that came in his way he cast aside; he refused to bow his head to anyone. He not only snubbed the aristocracy, but, according to the questionable testimony of Bettina Brentano, lectured to Goethe who did not do the same. But can we say that Beethoven truly disliked the well-mannered royalty? Oh no; not at all. This was but a repetition of his false attitude toward Napoleon. He liked them with the hullabaloo they raised over him; besides, they were valuable stepping-stones toward his goal. Although he detests all forms of formality, he never forgets to address the Archduke Rudolphas "Your Royal Highness," or to sign himself, "Your most humble and obedient servant." However, if he were to follow his natural impulses, he would probably open up the palace doors of "His Royal Highness," poke his head in between the doors, and yell at him, as he once did at Prince Lichnowsky, "Donkey!" But he must refrain from doing this, because the aristocracy can be of use to him. "They are only valuable instruments on which I play to suit my wants," he once said to Zmeskall. But bow to them? Never! Who are they that he, Beethoven, should bow to them? Besides, in his heart of hearts, he cannot tolerate them because they bear marks of distinction which he does not. And these marks of distinction are also signs of power, no less than the victories of Napoleon. They accept him into their circles and treat him like a royal one; but his parents were simple folk: his mother was a cook, and his father a chapel singer, but a drunkard at leisure. Nevertheless, he thinks it nice to make a habit of falling in love with royal ladies; to win the heart of a common woman is in itself a great conquest to him: to win the heart of a Countess is a still greater one; and in the art of love, like in that of music, Beethoven always prefers the great conquests to the little ones. In other things, too, he is most ambitious. In his latter years he is no longer content with dedicating his works to princes, so he ends by dedicating his "Ninth Symphony" to the King of Prussia. He hopes thereby to procure a generous order for his masterpiece, but receives only a ring in return. A ring! What use has the pretty Beethoven for ornaments? He is miserably disappointed. So he refuses to take the ring, and lo! his democratic principles come into play again. "I refuse to take presents from tyrants," he says. And we are almost inclined to believe him. To dedicate a masterpiece to a tyrant is not at all improper; but to accept gifts from him, and especially worthless ones, is not so good.

The true Beethoven has no political ideals, democratic or otherwise. Whatever ideas he has, he changes from day to day to suit himself. It is as impossible to put a tag on him as on the capricious Byron. If he chooses, he will insult the aristocracy to-day and play friends with them to-morrow. He tears off the title-page to "Eroica" on hearing that his hero has proclaimed himself emperor, and renounces him as a tyrant; yet, for all his anger and stampings, he still admits that Napoleon is his ideal of greatness, and writes: "Dedicated to the memory of a great man." This is only an indirect way of saying what he does not wish to admit to others: that Napoleon is still a great man, although he is a tyrant. Seventeen years later, when he hears that the Little Corsican has died at St. Helena, he can still say, "A long time ago I composed the music for that event," referring, of course, to the Funeral March of the "Eroica."

What is the sad result of all this? Firstly, we must conclude that Beethoven, in spite of his unique genius, was as much a hero-worshipper as the most common of us. He who, in his letter to his "Immortal Beloved," wrote, "The humility of man to man—it pains me," probably must have felt the truth of his own statement more than once. However, we can forgive this idolatry in him when we realize that it was merely a case of one powerful soul feeling strongly attracted toward another; or better still, the envious love of a creative angel for a destroying one.

The second outcome of Beethoven's love of Napoleon, however, cannot be so readily overlooked. All the anecdotes connected with the "Eroica" have proven a paradise for romantic programme inventors. With Beethoven's comments as sufficient justification for their erroneous notions, they usually begin by outlining the following program: The first movement of the "Eroica" as a description of Napoleon's life and battles. The second, a description of his funeral. The third, a description of the festivities that are wont to occur after the burial of the dead, more in concordance with ancient than with modern custom. The fourth—. But here they pause, and can find no definite programs for what they consider to be an unfitting group of variations. Why do they consider the variations unfitting? There are those who believe that the "Third" symphony should have ended like the "Fifth"—with a jubilant outburst equal in power to the preceding three movements. Those who believe this may, or may not, be justified. On the other hand, there are those who believe that the variations are unfitting merely because they had been looking forward to a suitable conclusion to the preceding programmatic descriptions. This is the danger that arises when a composer says too much about the origin of his own work. There are still millions of music lovers who cannot conceive of any other meaning for the first movement of the "Fifth" symphony than that of fate knocking at the door, an interpretation which Beethoven himself is said to have remarked to his factotum, Schindler. As a matter of fact, the first movement may represent any one of a host of battles besides those between man and fate. The picture is varied according to one's individual imagination; and that is precisely as it should be. To say that the "Funeral March" of the "Eroica" is nothing more than a description of the funeral of Napoleon, or of Moses, or of Beethoven himself, is like belittling the sublime aspects of the winds. The climax is approached and then allowed to die away, like shining hopes fading away in the far distance. But hark! As from the high mountain-top the hero-theme is ushered in again. There is a rugged splendor in it. A wise critic once said, "Never is Beethoven more a magician than when he takes up the horn"; and this statement is especially applicable to this masterly use of the horn in the first movement. It is to appear again, in the trio of the scherzo. In the meanwhile, we approach the wonderful coda breathlessly. It is broad, rugged, immense; being one of the new features of Beethoven's second period. As the movement closes, we seem to stagger with the glory that has come upon us, and we may well recall the words of Keats,

> Was it a vision or a waking dream?
> Fled is that music:—do I wake or sleep?

We have listened to the life and battles of the entire universe. The single man sinks into insignificance beside the vastness of all striving mortals. Truly has Beethoven spoken in his very own voice, and this time it was neither the adorned language of Haydn, nor the divine utterances of Mozart: it was a revelation from his own soul, and an echo of our own unspoken thoughts.

Second Movement: Marcia funèbre: adagio assai

This is the greatest epic of sorrow ever created in music. Mighty and terrifying is the funeral march from Wagner's "Götterdämmerung," which accompanies the slain Siegfried to his last resting-place; austere and forbidding, yet childishly hopeful is the celebrated funeral march from Chopin's "B flat minor sonata"; and the most noble resignation and godlike solemnity breathe forth from the pages of the funeral march from Schumann's "E flat piano quintet"; but this dirge by Beethoven is the apotheosis of alternating sorrow and hope, of despair and courage, of death and the life beyond. Here we do not find sorrow deserted by hope, as in the most characteristic pages of Tchaikovsky; neither do we encounter those heavenly smiles through tears, as we are wont in the flowing lyricism of Schubert; but here all elements of sorrow are no sooner expressed in their fullest and most inexhaustible state, than they are immediately redeemed by the most exalted and celestial hopes. These are notes which penetrate to the very core of the whole of suffering humanity; their untold sublimities are as vast and spacious as the earth itself; it is like the descent of the heavens to embrace the creatures of the soil. Nowhere in Beethoven's symphonies is he more the understanding sage and philosopher than in this majestic message. Let the humiliated genius listen to this, and he will feel his hatred toward his fellow creatures turn into pity; let the man of sweeter character, who sees the manifold flaws of the human race, listen to this, and he will shed a few tears for imperfections which cannot be corrected and which must remain as the eternal curse of mankind; let the man who overestimates his importance listen, and Nature will show him his humble place; and let the weary laborer surrender himself to this music, and he shall be comforted and made whole, and his weariness will suddenly appear like a blessing. For the greatness of this music lies in the fact that it contains something for everybody; it is the universal voice of comfort sounding to all corners of the earth. Were all the earth to die; were all life to be extinguished on, and within the earth; were all breathing organisms to die out in the air and in the seas; were all the earth nothing more but a dead body laid waste by some cataclysm; and could this globe yet continue its rotation around the sun, no music of the spheres could better bewail such destruction than this colossal and uplifting music by Beethoven.

What is sorrow, Beethoven seems to ask. Does it belittle man? And his reply seems to be: Sorrow can be as majestic as joy, as mighty as power, and as all-embracing as life itself. He shows us that man even in his most poignant grief can still be dignified. He seems to reassure us that human suffering does not belittle man, but rather strengthens him and brings him nearer to the divine. It is the light that helps him forward with greater maturity of purpose, as well as with more humility. It comes to him first as his enemy, then becomes his friend and teacher. To live is to know sorrow. Then let man accept his sufferings with godlike resignation, and peace shall be his ultimate reward.

The main theme with which the funeral march opens is one of heroic mournfulness. There is a sublime solemnity in it which fills us with awe and dread. If we close our eyes and surrender ourselves to it utterly, we may visualize black throngs of people marching after a grand hearse. They move slowly, and we can hear the shuffling of their feet. Their heads are bowed, but they cannot weep. Only the clouded skies, which hang low over their heads, are witness to their sorrow. But now the theme of hope comes upon us like the flooding rays of the sun. "Lift up your heads unto the skies," Beethoven seems to say, "and there you shall find peace and courage." This is like the smiling gaze of the heavens; the angelic utterance of one made pure by sorrow. About twenty-five years later we encounter such heavenly hope in the second theme of Chopin's funeral march, like an echo of what has gone before. As we continue, we are left stunned and terror-stricken. The oboe subject in the trio is the final word in redeeming eloquence. As the main theme is taken up again, the crowds, who have been silent in their grief up to now, seem to burst out in a violent protest against destiny. They seem to wring their hands and cry out, in the tones of the glorious fugato, "Why, O why?" And amid their tones of anguish, one seems to hear their sobs, which fill their bosoms to the point where words are suffocated before they are uttered. They advance with heavy footsteps, as though threatening the terrible force of death. Silence. No answer. Destiny remains unshaken and looks on with disturbing, Sphinx-like silence. The anguish of the people dying away, the main theme is ushered in again. It is the only reply to a mute inquiry: "It must be so." But now we are uplifted by the ethereal message of consolation at the beginning of the wondrous coda. Truly there is peace and rest in resignation. For a brief moment the very heavens are laid open to our gaze, and we catch a glimpse of regions of mellowed light. We are then led into the coda, wherein man's resistance against the inevitable slowly dies away and dissolves itself into the heavy laden air. Slowly, and with more weary tread, we are introduced to the main theme again. The people are tired of their grief. The theme ends brokenly, with uneven beats. It dies away…but not altogether. A last poignant groan pierces the air: the expiring breath of the colossal universe. In that one groan of anguish Beethoven's whole life of suffering is outpoured. It is the groan of one made great by sorrow, but of one who, for all his greatness, is only a man.

Third Movement: Scherzo e trio: allegro vivace

The contrast between the second and third movements of the "Eroica" is one of the most extreme transitions in all music. It is here, more than in any other symphony, that Beethoven shows himself to be a supreme optimist. The finale of the "Fifth Symphony," for instance, does not take us so completely by surprise, for we have already encountered Beethoven's optimism in the uplifting second theme of the preceding andante con moto. Neither are we amazed by the transition of the adagio andante into the finale of the "Ninth Symphony," for the previous scherzo has already prepared us for the joyous commotion of the introduction into the last movement, and the heavenly adagio was itself a foreboding of triumphant joy. As for the "Eighth Symphony," it is joyous throughout, as are the first and last two movements of the "Seventh." But here, in the "Eroica," we are taken completely by surprise. The allegro con brio was crowded with tumultuous conflicts, while the marcia funèbre spoke of melancholy and hope. Its moments of joy, when they appeared, were soft and subdued, like gentle moonbeams shedding their radiance through clouded skies; and not once was there a hint of the boisterousness of the third movement. In the scherzo we are at once lifted up out of our dejection and thrown headlong into a whirlpool of joy. The reaction is healthful both for our minds and bodies, and we come to regard Beethoven's delicious unexpectedness as a heavenly boon. Whenever we think of poor Mozart, who died at the very prime of his life, we should be thankful that he never lived to hear this scherzo, or his sensitive ears might have been greatly injured. For Mozart's joy differed from Beethoven's inasmuch as it was always angelic, whereas Beethoven's was always titanic. When Beethoven begins having fun, he sweeps everything out of the way, and laughs with a boisterousness loud enough to compare it with the rumbling of a volcano. As he lowers one down into the very depths of despair, so does he lift one up to the most mountainous peaks of jubilation. He does everything with the greatness of an intellectual giant, and makes it difficult for one to keep up with him. For genius is too impetuous for the world: it is always running ahead, with the rest of the world far behind.

This scherzo is epoch-making. Never before have we encountered such broadness, such vivacity, such utter individuality in the third movement of a symphony. It is the complete unloosening of all man's pent-up emotions like a swollen river overflowing its banks; it is the first of those gigantic bursts of life whose highest state is reached in the scherzo of the "Ninth Symphony." It is symbolic of the change that occurs in the outside world after the death of a great man. Time, which stands still for no one, continues on and on; and there is a gap left in the course of events which must be filled at once. A change occurs; new ideas rush in to take the place of old ones; there is a universal disturbance before everything settles down into its secure place again. Such was the tumult which Beethoven himself created with this glorious symphony, and which ushered in a new era of art at the beginning of the nineteenth century. After his death, the artistic discord was as great as the harmony had been during his life; a gap was open again, and composers rushed frantically to take up the threads where he had left off. But far from attaching this analysis to the scherzo as the only one possible, I say that there are dozens of other explanations equally fitting. I merely speak of what it brings to my own mind; and yet the images that crowd upon the imagination on hearing this music leave no space for a single interpretation. It would be folly to place a label on this, or on any other great work of art. Music, before all other arts, is the one language that is universal, and to label it is to belittle it. One may speak of what its varied moods bring to one's own mind, but only an ignorant and arrogant person would expect all others to share his own opinions. We shall deal with this further in our discussion of programme music.

From the invigorating vivacity of the main theme of the scherzo, we are led into the middle section for horns. This is one of the most delightfully rural passages in all of Beethoven's symphonies. Critics have called it a mere hunting call, but to my mind it is far from being only that. For it is here that we encounter Beethoven's genuine love of his fellow-men—a vast, child-like, all-embracing love. For at heart he is not the solitary, misanthropic personage his biographers have often pictured him to be, but a man who must forsake society although he loves it. He himself has said in his Heiligenstadt Testament:

> O Divine Being, Thou Who lookest down
> into my inmost soul, Thou understandest;
> Thou knowest that love for mankind and
> a desire to do good dwell therein.

Here we feel it, this very love of mankind of which he writes. Although given out by the horns, the trio is as much a drinking song as one of hunting. There is a warm and whole-hearted feeling of brotherhood in it. It is like a drink out of Keats's

...beaker full of the warm South,
Full of the true, the blushful Hippocrene,
With beaded bubbles winking at the brim,
And purple stained mouth.

We are to hear more of this in the trios of the third movements of the "Fourth," "Seventh," and "Ninth" symphonies. In the meanwhile, the main theme returns, bringing the scherzo to a joyous and typically Beethovenish conclusion.

Finale: Allegro molto

Few of Beethoven's works have been as misjudged as the finale of the "Eroica." As we have already seen, this is partly due to the erroneous series of descriptions tagged on to the previous movements. This is one of the belittling qualities of word pictures, when their purpose is to describe music. The abstract becomes the concrete, and the universal art of music is no longer what it should be.

The finale of the "Eroica" is one of those things in art which one will fail to comprehend until one knows it as well as one does oneself. One must not listen to it for the sake of comparing it with the previous movements, but it must be regarded as a complete structure by itself. The apotheosis of conflict, sorrow, hope, and rejoicing ended with the completion of the scherzo; the finale is not a fulfillment, as we might aptly call the finale of the "Fifth Symphony," but a reconsideration of all that has gone before. Without putting any positive label on it, we may nevertheless regard it as a series of afterthoughts. We do not know what prompted Beethoven to write it in that style, but we may suppose that it may have originated from his inborn desire toward innovations. The first movement of the "Eroica," with its colossal broadness and hitherto unheard-of titanic expressions of independence, is in itself a monumental masterpiece of innovation. The second movement is not less revolutionary, for never before had a funeral march been written as the slow movement of a symphony. The third movement is perhaps the most unique innovation of all, for here the first of Beethoven's scherzos appears on a giant scale. Perhaps, with all these gigantic innovations, Beethoven experienced an abhorrence toward the conventional quick movement of the finale. Or perhaps, with his customary unexpectedness at the last moment, he decided to play a little prank and amuse himself with what the critics would say. If such was the case, Beethoven's little prank had tremendous consequences, for critics have degraded it until the present day. So strikingly convincing and direct is the finale of the "Fifth Symphony," which Beethoven wrote some years later, that, by its very forcefulness it created the unchangeable impression that all symphonies should end triumphantly. Hence we see how even a unique master work can, through no fault of its own, produce improper impressions. Let us therefore not deplore the finale of the "Eroica," but rather the public's attitude toward it.

The superb series of variations of the finale begins with a towering introduction. The plucking of the strings which follows is pregnant with sinister expectation, and Brahms probably thought of it in the finale of his "First Symphony." The variations commence, and soon we are introduced to the Prometheus theme, which is like the bearing of good tidings of joy. Again and again the theme occurs, always returning to the bass. Here in the very manner in which the theme constantly reappears, does Beethoven seem to reconsider the philosophy of the previous movements. There is something about them which suggests going forth, a forward march of all the generations and climes which ultimately bring all things into their proper places. The programme-maker may go so far as to say that these variations are consistent with the previous movements, and that they represent a marching by of the years, which eventually bring fame and glory to the bewept hero of the funeral march. Nowhere is even the most violent opposer to programmes more apt to feel the possible truth of such an interpretation than toward the close where the theme is given out in the woodwind instruments. There is a quality about this final appearance of the theme which suggests that the marching years can now be seen only from a distance, and that they are casting reproachful looks at us and bidding us farewell. Be the matter as it may, there is a healing note of finality in this slowing up of the Prometheus theme which suggests that there is great peace in reaching one's ultimate conclusion about things. I can think of few places as thrilling as the bridge between this and the final outburst, which sends us whirling into the jubilant coda. This introduction is crowded with forebodings such as even the greatest feel before their final victory. The coda does not come as a surprise, but it leaves us dizzy with ecstasy. It is like a great rocking of the world, which is finished too soon for one to realize one has heard it. Thus does Beethoven carry himself, no less than us, to victory; and still the glories of the "Eroica" are not exhausted. For they are endless; as vast as the earth; as significant as truth; and as eternal as life itself.

The Fourth Symphony in B Flat, Opus 60

On Schumann's statement about the Fourth Symphony

Schumann's critical statement about the "Fourth Symphony" is one of the most misleading things ever written about it. It is difficult to believe that the same man who had so cleverly spoken of the "heavenly length" of Schubert's "C major symphony" should so erroneously have referred to Beethoven's "Fourth Symphony" as "a slender Greek maiden between two Norse giants." The "two Norse giants," are, of course, the "Third" and "Fifth" symphonies which Schumann named most appropriately. In my opinion, however, the "Fourth Symphony," far from resembling "a slender Greek maiden," is one of the most virile creations that ever came from Beethoven's pen. Had Schumann referred only to the introduction to the first movement, and to the heavenly adagio, his words might have been more fitting; but he was so completely carried away by the beauty of these very parts, that he quite forgot the vigor of the succeeding ones. Just as soon could one term the whole "Ninth Symphony" angelic and Shelley-like because of its adagio. Every moment of Beethoven's symphonies is so crowded with beauties of its own, that we quite forget everything else while listening to it. In our attempt to express our emotions, we sometimes overstep all bounds, and then find that even that has been in vain. For beauties such as Beethoven's cannot be named; they must only be accepted. Even so do we gaze up at the evening star, and the fact that it is the evening star does not add to its celestial beauty.

First Movement: Adagio; allegro vivace

The symphony begins with a mystic introduction which harmonizes more with the second movement than with the first. It is like the shades of departed spirits moving through underground regions. Through the darkness we seem to catch faint rays of light, which leads us forward toward some unseen destination. Perhaps it is

Beethoven himself who is groping onward toward the light. With typically Beethovenish abruptness we are led into the main theme. If this symphony reflects Beethoven's love for the Countess Therese von Brunswick, as some biographers have claimed, this principle theme of the first movement is surely a most abundant revelation of the overrunning wells of Beethoven's sexual nature. Such vigor is the last word in virility; and such restless happiness and complete abandonment to the simpler joys of living is seldom encountered in any of Beethoven's later works. Here we do not find any forebodings of the titanic paeans of joy which are later to ring out in the finale of the "Fifth Symphony"; but warm, healthful good humor, and a refreshing exuberance of spirits. As Romain Rolland has so aptly said, "The lion is in love, and draws in his claws." But far from only drawing in his claws, he does not even once show his fangs. If he roars occasionally, it is only like a sleepy growl; and we are almost inclined to say, "Growl again, Beethoven."

Second Movement: Adagio

Yes; Beethoven is in love: the first movement has awakened our suspicions; the second confirms them. The main theme is one of such serene and romantic beauty, that to drink it in fully is to become a poet oneself. Its loveliness is so deep that it pains one to listen to it. It seems to have the fragrance of summer rose buds and honeysuckle. This heavenly theme is accompanied by a continuous rhythmic figure which emphasizes the poetic longing of the principle melody. There is a delicious monotony in it which lulls one to sleep. It is altered from time to time, and is finally transferred to the drums with growing intensity, like the persistent beating of the heart which quickens with the growing disturbance of man's erotic senses. Few things in all symphonic literature are more exquisite. One is reminded of Shelley's rapturous Indian serenade, written in honor of an adored one. From tender love we mount to glowing passion, and thence to the full consummation of all inner longings. This is Beethoven's supreme jest at his unfulfilled love-life. "Poor Beethoven," he was to write some years later, after her, the middle-aged man had been rejected by the fifteen-year-old Therese Malfatti; "there is no happiness for you in this world; only in the realms of the ideal will you find strength to conquer yourself."

And the adagio of the "Fourth Symphony" is the realm of Beethoven's ideal: it is the love which he always sought, but which he never found, save in his strangely mystic dreams. He was soon to come to the fullest realization of the fact that "the elect among men draw bliss out of their sufferings." Now he is only smiling—a warm, serene smile, with his firm teeth showing. At times he grows pensive, like a faun musing among the ruins of ancient temples in fallen Greece; but youth, his supreme comforter, is still with him, and soothes his wearied brow. The sunshine of life is still upon him; the purple mantle of night is yet to come.

Third Movement: Minuetto: Allegro vivace

The lover's vigor re-awakens. Sleep and pleasant dreams have given him added vitality. After the boisterousness of the opening theme, a tender trio appears, like the woods echoing man's poetic emotions. There is exquisite beauty in this, and at the same time a quaint simplicity which captivates one. It is a theme of universal love and friendship, such as we have already encountered in the horn sections of the scherzo of the "Eroica." There is nothing that makes Beethoven quite as amiable as these droll and lazy trios. The main theme returns. Beethoven gives us a tiny slice of the trio again, as though he were going to begin it all over again; but we know his little tricks too well by this time. He gives us a sudden pound on our backs and takes leave of us with a good-natured grin. As Schumann has so well observed: it is only "just one more question for the horn to put" before Beethoven makes his final leap.

Fourth Movement: Allegro ma no troppe

There is a breeziness in this movement which almost makes us hold our hats down over our heads for fear they will blow away. There seems to be no end to the little skirmishes, which fill the heart with delight to the point of overflowing. Beethoven pokes his droll witticisms at us with an abundance which almost puts Voltaire to shame. All the same we are led to say to ourselves: "Poor Beethoven! Never again will he so completely brim over with jolly laughter." For even in the "Eighth Symphony" there is not such fine youthful fun. Yes, it is the spontaneous fun of youth, which nothing can withhold. It is like a round of perpetual motion, and it makes us sigh that it should end. But even the mischievous winds of March must disappear, and the eddies of sand must settle in their places again. Even so is the main subject enlarged, only to die away in the violins and bassoons. Beethoven's dreams of love were to die away likewise, and become one with the dying wind. All too soon is fate to come knocking at the door.

THE FIFTH SYMPHONY IN C MINOR, OPUS 67

First Movement: Allegro con brio

Nowhere, except in the titanic opening of the "Ninth Symphony," is Beethoven more the colossal giant than in the first movement of the "Fifth Symphony." True, the first movement of the "Eroica" contains an interweaving of themes and a structural broadness that is epoch-making; but in the first movement of the "C minor symphony" we encounter powers all the more gigantic because of their very directness and seeming spontaneity. The heroic strength of this movement seems quite as natural as the very thunderings of the heavens, or the impetuous rushing of the ocean. Should we listen to it during a lightning storm, the very elements will seem belittled when compared with the grandeur of the music. It is not an imitation of any particular elemental or emotional conflict; it is rather the sublimation of them all. There is an element of relentless fury in it that fills one with the wonder of beholding creative miracles; it is like Hercules shaking his iron fist at the heavens, or like the echoing roars of a wounded lion. At times it seems like the voice of genius shouting out against universal neglect and humiliation; and, if for a moment it assumes milder tones, its wrath is all the greater afterward. We may listen to other music many times, and soon it will lose some of its power; but the rugged strength of the first movement of the "Fifth Symphony" always comes upon one so suddenly that one's consciousness is left paralyzed, and hardly do one's senses awaken than the music is at an end. One may surrender oneself to it fully, and yet never completely become part of it, for it frightens rather than reassures one. "My God!" exclaimed Goethe, on merely hearing Mendelssohn's piano arrangement of the score, "it is great, stupendous!" And then he was to cry again, "*Und wenn das alle die Menschen zusammen spielen!*" (And suppose the whole world played it together!) The dignified creator of "Faust" turned aghast from this heaven-storming madness. Years later it was to frighten Tolstoy as well, and the author of "The Kreutzer Sonata" was to find Beethoven "unnatural." A famous actress was to go into convulsions on hearing it performed for the first time; while Berlioz, swept away by its tempestuous power, was to hasten out into the open air in order to breathe more freely and regain his senses. Truly this music is as wonderful and unexplainable as life, and as terrifying and mysterious as death and the unknown world beyond. It is earthly, yet it is in a superior attitude to the heavens. Never for a moment is the music anyone's but Beethoven's, and that alone is the secret of its eternal power. For Beethoven is strength; and strength is the keynote to this most heroic of musical utterances.

The movement opens with its famous four notes, of which, according to the questionable testimony of Schindler, Beethoven is supposed to have remarked: "Thus does fate knock at the door." On these four notes the entire movement is built. Nowhere have we a more characteristic example of Beethoven's genius for building colossal worlds out of nothingness. We are left stunned by the walls that seem to rise and fall above us; we are left breathless as the elements are lashed into fury and we become one with the outer forces. In our amazement we think we are beholding some terrible phenomenon, and we feel like one who turns his eyes away from some forbidden spectacle on the high seas. This is a manifestation of such power as might have staggered the ancient gods; it almost makes Michelangelo's Medici figures appear like statuettes. Only one of the truly giant minds of all time could have conceived music like this. We little wonder, on hearing this, why some practical-minded people come to regard Beethoven as one who dwelt with the gods. For this is music that paralyzes one's sense of reason; to listen to it and absorb it fully is to begin to believe in those very things which one's calm intelligence denies.

The second theme is one of the most sublime Beethovenish glimpses into purer worlds of beauty. After the struggles of the human or elemental forces, rest always follows; be it the rest of a moment, or the rest of a day, it always comes like a heavenly boon. But let us observe how short this divine comfort is ere it undergoes a transition to a higher plane and bursts out in jubilation. For hope always brings with it visions of ultimate triumph and victory. In one's intense desire to reach out toward the heavens and subdue them within the heroic elements of one's own soul, one's hand is stayed for a moment with the full realization of one's comparative insignificance, but the very pause gives one additional strength, and new-born sensations of vigor surge within the blood. The battle begins anew—the battle to thrust one's self forward, if even at the impossible. And so does it continue until the end, when the fate theme is renewed again, only to conclude abruptly, like the vibration of a giant hammer which strikes against an entire world made of steel.

Second Movement: Andante con moto

The second movement is one of the most heavenly conceptions in all music. It is not less peaceful and hopeful than the previous one was turbulent and overbearing. The chief theme has a sublimity in it that is distinctly pastoral. It is like one of Shelley's abstract contemplations on the beauties of the universe, while gazing up at the evening star. The second theme is one of majestic grandeur and nobility—like the opening of the heavens amid a flare of trumpets. One is reminded of those oblique floods of lights which are depicted in the holy pictures of the early masters, and which shed radiance over some sacred person or object. Let us observe with what infinite fondness Beethoven caresses and fondles these two themes; there is something of Schubertian persistency in the sublime variations, which expand the heart with a thousand emotions of pity and tenderness. Toward the end Beethoven gives us a prophetic glimpse into the modern world of jazz, which causes our single smile of amusement throughout the entire movement of untold sublimities. The ending has a note of decision in it which only Beethoven could have expressed with such dramatic abruptness. It leaves us in the air, rather than on the earth; and we are at once prepared for still greater things to come.

Thus does man wander forth into the woods to find rest from his endless battles. But peace does not come all at once, so that it may be sweeter when it ultimately arrives.

Third Movement: Scherzo e trio, which runs directly into the Finale: Allegro; return of trio from previous movement; and final presto

Before the light comes the darkness. There is a mysterious introduction leading into the principle subject. The main theme appears, like a spectre of the past coming to haunt one at midnight. It is an echo of the fate theme of the first movement, but whereas previously it was purely a symbol of giant force, now it is one of argumentative reconsideration. We are introduced to the quaintly humorous and droll fugato which has a certain measure of impish impetuosity in it. Never did Beethoven seem more full of boisterous fun. This supplies a much needed period of relief from the suspense that preceded it, and from that which is to follow. The plucking of the strings on the return of the main theme arouses our suspense to the point where the very atmosphere seems to grow dense. It is a conspiracy in whispers. What are they plotting, these unseen spirits? Slowly the wondrous bridge is begun, which is to lead us into the finale. The sustained chord on the strings is accompanied by the persistent tapping of the drums, which gradually increases in intensity. This miraculous bridge is not only one of the most highly inspired moments in all symphonic literature, but one of the most colossal inspirations in all art. Here we feel the beginning of that stupendous influence which was to lead Liszt to the conception of his tone-poem, with its continuous series of poetic pictures. We must not make the error of concluding, however, that Beethoven built this unique bridge with the sole purpose of doing what no other had done before him. So heavy is the suspense with which the third movement is laden, that to have cut it short in the conventional manner would have been for Beethoven to have cut the thread he had so cautiously been weaving. So akin is the entire symphony to the elemental wonders of nature, that one cannot expect it to follow standards of any sort. It is as natural for the third movement to lead directly into the fourth as it is for an explosion to follow the rumbling in a volcano. Bearing this in mind, let us observe the stupendous C major chord which terminates this bridge. Where can we find anything to measure up to it? Should we recall that jubilant outburst in Haydn's "Creation" symbolizing the appearance of light, or the equally wonderful C major chord before the coda of Weber's overture to

"Der Freischütz," we will find that Beethoven's introduction of the colossal chord is even more wonderful because of the very greatness of his preparation for it. In the outburst on "light" in the "Creation," our only preparation for the outburst were the words themselves, "And there was...". In the overture to "Der Freischütz" the chord was sounded out of darkness and the light. In the "C minor symphony," however, the preparation for the outburst is such a certain and unmistakable one, that the C major chord seems to follow only as a matter of course. This is the great secret of all supreme art: that all its effects seem so timely that we accept them not as wonderful things we have never seen or heard before, but as things that exist for no other reason than that they cannot do otherwise.

Nowhere in the entire field of instrumental music can we find a more perfect outburst of joy than in the finale into which we are now introduced. As music of the highest triumphant ecstasy and titanic rapture it stands as high in the symphonic field as the "Hallelujah Chorus" of Handel's "Messiah" stands among the entire literature of religious music. It is so breath-taking in its fiery intensity, so spontaneous in its jubilation, so dramatic in its overpowering effects, and, above all, so startlingly and brutally direct, that one may well say that it is not the work of a mere genius, but of a human colossus. It is a towering and irrepressible fountain of joy; a surging ocean of euphonious rhythm, with waves breaking against happy shores. It is here, more than in any other work, that Beethoven reveals himself as being a genuine optimist at heart. The brooding despondency of the Heiligenstadt Testament; his endless complaints against the bitterness and cruelties of existence; his egotistical attitude which often made him believe that he was singled out from all men to bear the burdens of the universe;—all these impressions of his pessimism are dwarfed when placed side by side with his gigantic expression of man's optimism in the finale of this symphony. Just as soon could a real pessimist have written this music as an atheist could have composed "The Messiah." Let us recall, when we hear this outburst of optimism, that it was written by the self-same man who, only nine days before his death, wrote:

Wonderful! Wonderful! Wonderful!
I shall be saved solely by Dr. Malfatti's skill!

But before all else, let us recall that Beethoven's very life is the sole proof of his optimism. He lived only because his genius was greater than his sufferings, and because his desire to live was greater than his desire to die. This is one of the many hopeful messages of the C minor symphony.

The opening theme is one of broad, majestic triumph. Wagner may have felt the influence of this in his lordly opening of the overture to "Die Meistersinger," as Schubert probably had before him in the colossal opening of the finale of the "C major symphony." "*Ah, c'est l'empereur!*" (Ah, it is the emperor!), a Parisian of the Old Guard exclaimed on first hearing it performed in Vienna. And indeed, it is one of the most kingly passages of dignified joy in all music. We are swept along until the main theme of the previous movement re-enters. There is an unmistakable psychological explanation for this repetition. Beethoven was philosopher enough to understand that man's greatest triumphs are ever and anon interrupted by his recollections of the bitter past. Even so did Jeanne d'Arc, having raised the siege of Orleans, sit and weep over the memory of the men her armies had killed. It is a feeling as common to the lowly as to the great. But Beethoven's triumph is too great to be marred for too long a time, so his recollections slip into the background again, and once more he surrenders himself wholeheartedly to his joy. The principle theme recurs, but it is to be noted that this time the bridge on which it re-enters is shorter than the previous one at the beginning of the movement, and the huge chord on which the bridge terminates is not as colossal or sustained as previously. Beethoven is too well aware of the greatness of what he has already done for him to cheapen it by a deliberate repetition. With bold decision he brings us nearer to the end, for too much joy, like too much wine, is unhealthful. The movement approaches its close on a tumultuous wave of universal joy, in which all voices seem to rise in one grand paean of triumph; and thus one of the most glorious human documents is concluded.

THE SIXTH SYMPHONY IN F, OPUS 68 "THE PASTORAL"

On Programme Music

A subtle man once said that Wagner has been abused because he is too sublime. Of Beethoven's "Sixth Symphony" one might likewise say that it has been abused because it is too beautiful. Save for its first movement, it is not abstract music; that is true enough. It is music with a distinct, concrete meaning. What is more, Beethoven labeled all the movements. He must have done so with great misgiving, for, in order to convince himself, no less than his audiences that the symphony was not a mere series of tone pictures, he wrote on the title page, "Pastoral Symphony, or a recollection of country life. More an expression of feeling than tone-painting." We must smile on reading this statement. Beethoven was making a dangerous experiment,[1] but he was very cautious lest the abuse of posterity rain down on his head. Things have come about precisely as he foresaw, for Beethoven was a prophet in this, as in other things.

What do critics condemn in the "Sixth Symphony"? Firstly, they point out that music is the most universal of arts and should therefore not be degraded by concrete meanings. There is some justification in this; but critics, picture a conflict which Beethoven did not intend? Shall we say that the ending of Liszt's "Les Preludes" is not glorious merely because to some it does not seem like the ascension of the soul into paradise? Or lastly, shall we take Shubert's dramatic gem, "The Erl-King," and say that it is not a lyric masterpiece merely because it does not happen to bring Goethe's poem to our minds? A great work cannot be elevated or belittled by an individual impression of its significance; it always stands on one plane, and the public's reception of it is not always a revelation of the art's own worth, but more often of the keenness, or on the other hand, the dullness of those who criticize it. Only those of broad and lofty intellect can view beauty for its own beautiful sake; but these few

36

are so greatly in the minority, that music must retain its programmatic notes if it is to belong to the universe and not to the elevated few.

There is also this factor to be considered: that, provided the listener's mind can follow the composer's programmatic notes, and that his mind is wholly in harmony with them, does he really lose anything? The truth is that he will lose very little, if anything at all. It will only make the Brook Scene of the "Sixth Symphony" appear all the lovelier, since the composer has reassured the listener that it is a brook and nothing else which he is listening to. Minds which are not of the highest musical maturity must react like this; but as long as it adds to the beauty of their conceptions, it is not to be condemned. As Keats has said, "Beauty is truth," and this maxim is as applicable to art as to life. There are all sorts of minds: therefore there must be all sorts of standards. We can just as soon expect an ordinary person to react toward musical ideas with the same abstract broadness of an intellectual as we could have expected Beethoven's factotum, Schindler, to act and think like Beethoven. To take all programs away, therefore, is as extreme a danger as to have them present at every possible musical occasion. Programs should be handed out with moderation, read with moderation, and considered with moderation. Those who must respond to them, will do so; those who do not need them will dispose of them, or better still, eye them with curiosity; and each man will have the satisfaction of thinking his own attitude the only correct one. For even in the judgement of one's own self men have their standards.

First Movement: Allegro ma non troppo, "Joyous sensations aroused by arrival in the country"

The principle theme of this movement seems to smell of morning meadows and dewy rosebuds. One can almost feel the odor of the damp, black soil. Throughout there is the languorous feeling that comes with the long summer days. Deliciously sweet twitterings assail our ears from all sides; now and then we hear faint horn calls, accompanied by the gentle rustling of the leaves. We know that we are in a paradise of pastoral loveliness. At times we fancy we can see gnomes peeking at us from behind aged oaks. All our rural fancies come to life. Every living thing seems to have a voice of its

37

own, and even the grass in which we tread seems to speak to us. When we think of Beethoven at this time, we picture him not as the mad, morose being who wrote the Heiligenstadt Testament, but as a man who was content even in his deafness. For here, as these gentle murmurings come to us, we picture a man whose inner ear was opened to all the varied concerts of nature. He could understand her language, and draw solace from her as few men of mere perfect hearing could. Did he himself not say that no man has ever loved the country more than he did?

Every tree seems to cry, 'Holy, holy!'

And that is what we feel in this movement of heavenly sounds; a feeling of holiness, as though everything, from the greatest to the smallest, were endowed with holy beauty. Beethoven's soul is in itself the most heavenly emblem of this eternal beauty. His is a beauty that casts its radiance over Nature herself, perfecting, rather than imitating her. For when we listen to this music, we may well say that Beethoven, like Shelley, stands trembling with rapture at the joyousness his soul has evoked. He seems to have become the truest seer of nature,—the truest because the simplest; and he seems so transported with joy that we can almost see him going to every tree and embracing each one separately, crying to them, "I love you, I love you—with all my heart and soul I love you." It is a love which is greater than Beethoven himself, and which is as beautiful as it is ennobling; for the moment Beethoven seems transfigured, even as Christ was on the Mount.

Second Movement: Andante molto moto, "Scene by the Brook"

Never was Beethoven's soul more transparently lovely than in this second movement. The full radiance of his poetic and childlike spirit shines throughout these notes like shining pebbles in crystal waters. So intimately does Beethoven acquaint us with the beauties of his subject, that a mere brook becomes an object of eternal significance. Where one false mote might have belittled the delicate subject, where one superficial or unnecessary idea might have marred the refined conception of this tonal poem, a highly masterful and poetic tone is maintained throughout. Let us observe the short introduction into the main theme, which is a mere slowing up of the principle theme of Handel's "Hallelujah Chorus." Even in this there is an angelic loveliness. The main theme appears, and its caressing simplicity and gently flowing rhythm is like a rapturous smile of a seraph. There is a languorousness, a delicious monotony in this, as well as in the following theme, which bring warmth and poetic reveries to one. One can almost feel the cool water rippling through one's partly closed fingers, and one's emotions seem to become part of the brook. The drowsy repetitions on the divided strings sound the gentler murmurs which one can barely hear, but which form an undercurrent to the beautiful whole. Nothing escapes Beethoven's attention; quite the contrary, he has been accused of being superfluous, if not superficial, toward the end when the famous, but much abused bird notes occur. Some critics have pointed out that when Beethoven introduced them he began that influence of exaggerated realism which was to find its maddest culmination in Respighi's "Pina di Roma," in which the composer used an actual gramophone recording of a nightingale's voice. Mr. Lawrence Gilman, a New York critic, compared this letter proceeding with that of a fanatic painter who, to satisfy his dreadful urge for realism, tears a leaf off a tree and glues it into his landscape canvas. Romain Rolland, who has always shown a rare and understanding sympathy toward great souls, came to Beethoven's rescue with the worthy excuse that the deaf master was only trying to recapture that which he used to hear in his better days. This is very possible, and, if such was the case, Beethoven must have derived considerable comfort from this pitiful source. If Beethoven was even remotely akin to the fanatic painter already mentioned, let us remember that a painter could commit the apparent folly of pasting a real leaf on his canvas, and yet, by his intuitive knowledge of just where to place the leaf, the true beauty of the canvas would not be marred to the outward eye. He will not only place the leaf where it is most fitting, but he will surround it with painted leaves no different in color, and he will give it a glimmer of sunshine that will make it appear more beautiful than it had been before. Fantastic and far-fetched as this may seem in painting, it is not so in music. Musicians, as well as artists of all sorts, may borrow from one another provided that they can enhance the beauty of what they borrow; why then is it wrong for a supreme genius like Beethoven to borrow from Nature herself, if he can bring new beauty and significance to his borrowings? The fact remains that Beethoven did not thrust the bird notes in at any untimely moment, but that he led up to them beautifully and with the utmost care. Let us recall, too, the fragrant loveliness of the melody that follows the first appearance of the bird notes like a heavenly refrain, and the closing repetition of the enchanting embellishment, which concludes the movement, and we shall understand that Beethoven took a soulless melody from Mother Nature and returned it to her not only with sweeter beauty, but with new poetic significance. It was like taking a diamond out of its natural bed and making it shine more brightly by cutting its sides and placing it in a setting of gold. So surpassing has the abundant loveliness of the movement been up to the closing bird notes, that Beethoven must have felt a sudden and irrepressible desire to conclude with a token of undisguised love for one of those many voices which he had hitherto only imitated. The concluding song of the bird must have been the outpouring of the gift which Mother Nature has so lavishly bestowed on him. And so it was that Beethoven no longer imitated Nature, but became one with her.

Third Movement: Allegro: "Merry gathering of country peasants, followed by Thunderstorm." This leads directly into the Fourth Movement: Allegretto: "Glad and grateful feelings after the storm."

Of the remaining parts of the "Sixth Symphony" some critics have spoken with not less scorn than of the bird episode in the brook scene. The peasant's merry-making has been called pure farce. For my part, I regard it as a further manifestation of the breadth of Beethoven's greatness. Let us recall the titanic happiness expressed in the finale of the "Fifth Symphony," and we shall feel that there Beethoven expressed the joy of supermen, not of simple people. That colossal outburst and revelry was purely Beethoven's own; could ordinary souls experience such mad ecstasy, it would be too great, too incomprehensible for them. Beethoven himself must have experienced such a jubilant surge of emotions on completing one of his masterpieces; Caesar must have felt it on making one of his conquests; but it most assuredly is not sane, normal happiness.

Ordinary people can listen to it and marvel at it only inasmuch as it represents something they have felt in the outer forces, or which they feel must exist in the world at large; it is akin to them only insofar as it is symbolic of their joy on a giant scale. The same is true of the vast majority of Beethoven's scherzos. In the third movement of the "Sixth Symphony," however, Beethoven comes down to earth and shows us that his soul is filled with as much love for ordinary peasants as for heaven-storming titans. It is the work of a man who loved Michelangelo, and who kept a bust of Brutus in his writing room, but who, for all his love toward intellectual superiority and idealistic beauty, yet could find joy in visiting a village tavern and sit four hours listening to the quaint performances of a group of common peasants. Not only did he listen to them with great eagerness, but composed dance music for them;—he, the transcendental genius and composer of the "Ninth Symphony"! Herein—in this very scherzo of the "Sixth Symphony"—Beethoven reveals this spaciousness of his loving heart. He comes intimately close to the common laborers of the earth and embraces them with healthy, whole-hearted vigor. For he who truly loves mankind, loves the simple as well as the great; and this is one of the very reasons why Beethoven's death-mask hangs in the homes of the humble, and why eyes are wont to meet the surface of the cold clay and rest on it with mild and appreciative expressions of gladness.

The opening theme of the third movement of the "Pastoral" is one of the most refreshing and exhilarating in all of Beethoven's symphonies. The whole movement is filled with quaint and lovable passages bubbling over with healthy fun. There is an exuberance of spirits in it, varying with passages of summery drowsiness. The second theme is one of the utmost simplicity, and one of Beethoven's most characteristic drolleries. As he goes romping back into the principle theme, the peasants seem to shout, "Now turn round!" This is followed by a theme of genuine Russian flavor, which adds to the general merriment. So infectious does this gaiety become, that we are tempted to rise and stamp our feet with the others. Suddenly, however, there is a pause. We are led directly into the thunderstorm. Rossini might have found an inspiration in this for the thunderstorm of his "William Tell Overture," as well as for the scene of peace which follows. But let us observe how differently Beethoven and Rossini evoke the elements. Rossini, having completed the first part of his overture, does not expand it directly into the second movement, but pauses and definitely starts a new movement before he begins the storm. Hence, by this very lack of subtlety, Rossini fails to reproduce the utter capriciousness of elemental disturbances. Nature does not wait until we have drunk in the full beauty of the outdoors before she begins her storm. Her awful power lies in her very tendency to surprise us at the most unexpected moment, as she does in the "Pastoral Symphony" when she interrupts the merrymaking with characteristic abruptness and sends everyone scurrying for shelter. Beethoven had too much of the elemental force of nature in himself for him to fail to realize that Nature does not pause at any time or moment for the benefit of people who happen to be making merry in the woods, but that she goes about her work independently of everybody. Liszt was to profit by this example in the superb conflict in "Les Preludes."

I have always been at a loss to understand why so many critics have referred to the thunderstorm as "a claptrap display" and "melodrama." Only lately, however, I concluded, as I have already said before, that their great knowledge of orchestral techniques is the sole explanation for these unjust phrases. They rely too much on their perfect knowledge of how certain effects are produced, for them to appreciate the effects for their sole sake. But let them forget what instruments Beethoven uses in producing his simple effects, and let them surrender themselves to the music with the full-hearted appreciation of mere children. They cannot fail to see that the thunderstorm Beethoven depicts is more awe-inspiring than an elemental storm itself. For one thing, it is a powerful expression of the disturbance which man is wont to experience within himself, and a fascinating revelation of man's will to subdue the outer forces. Anyone who has himself striven to get on an equal footing with Nature, cannot fail to feel elevated by this manifestation of Beethoven's sweeping power. That this is the work of a man is in itself a blessed revelation of the fact that the human race is not inferior to the elements, but that their power is merely of another sort. Hence this music, like nature herself, has a philosophical, as well as an artistic significance; and who can say if its former meaning is not superior to its latter one?

What shall we say of the fourth movement, which is supposed to reveal the "degenerated Beethoven"? It is one of the loveliest inspirations which ever dawned on a genius. Truly it is the sublimest of Wordsworth's odes to nature, translated into the poetry of music. The opening notes, which give us a view of the dark clouds fading away into smiling skies, are as sweet and wholesome as the very essence of Beethoven's childlike soul. It is to be noticed that Beethoven does not pause after the thunderstorm, but continues straight ahead as he had done before, thus preserving the perfect harmony of the whole. Just as nature had taken the peasants unawares and driven them out of the fields, so does she bring them back again, and without the least ceremony. The hymn of thanksgiving which is ushered in with the utmost beauty, is not so much a hymn of the peasants, as a song of brotherhood direct from Beethoven's heart. Once again we recall those delightful horn passages in the scherzo of the "Eroica," which bore a similar significance. Here Beethoven opens up his heart to the entire universe, and embraces his fellow creatures with a wholeheartedness and good humor that anticipates the all-embracing harmony of the joy theme from the finale of the "Ninth Symphony." Mendelssohn was to be tempted to an expression of similar beauty toward the end of his "Scotch Symphony," where, after the war-like rhythms of the allegro vivacissimo, he enters into the hymn-like serenity of the allegro maestoso assai. The sunny warmth of the tender variations is like a flood of sunbeams. I am reminded of one of Toscanini's incomparable renditions of the "Sixth Symphony" late in 1934 at Carnegie Hall in New York. As the auditorium was filled with the abundant beauty of the finale, the eyes of the audience instinctively turned upward, as though in anticipation of the sun which seemed on the verge of breaking in through the ceiling of the hall. For my own part, I have never heard this finale without having to rise and walk to the window, where I could gaze up at the serene skies. At those moments I have always felt intimately close to the happy pulse of the universe, and a full-hearted love toward all living things has always filled my heart. For this music is the sweet friend of all men, great and small; it purifies the heart, broadens the vision, and expands the sympathies. It is the message of one who has always sought Nature, and who has at last found her.

THE SEVENTH SYMPHONY IN A MAJOR, OPUS 92

On the General Attitude Toward the Seventh Symphony

T he "Seventh Symphony" is one of those works which contain such an abundance of beauty that one's sense of judgement is apt to fail if one compares it with other symphonies. It is a futile task to compare masterpieces, no less than to make comparisons among the shining splendor of the heavenly bodies. Within certain limits, however, comparisons can be made. Among the most mature works of Beethoven, one must fail to find a single symphony that is totally superior to another.[2] If the finale of the "Eroica" completely lacks in the spontaneity of the finale of the "Fifth Symphony," the slow movement of the "Fifth" does not measure up to the supreme sublimity of the funeral march of the "Third."

I have never been able to fully account for the fact that the public, as well as the majority of the critics, have placed the "Seventh Symphony" side by side with the "Eroica." These two works are so far apart in emotional content that comparisons between the two seem unthinkable. Whereas the "Eroica" is crowded with overpowering conflicts, the "Seventh" is essentially a rhythmic masterpiece. The "Eroica" is an epic poem of conflict and sorrow, redeemed by hope and the ultimate victory of the coda, while the "Seventh" is a poem of victory alone. I further fail to perceive "the sublimities" of the "Seventh Symphony," which some critics assign to it. Its allegretto, as I say later on, is far from being sublime; and its remaining three movements are the very essence of movement itself, but they are full of good-natured, bearish fun, rather than sublimity. Some may say that this is not consistent with my later statement in which I say that the fourth movement is "like the wild revelry of the drunken gods of Olympus"; but then the spectacle of drunken gods, could it be witnessed, would certainly not be a sublime one. The comparison is used with the sole purpose of emphasizing the general feeling of drunken frenzy which is present especially in the last movement of the symphony.

Another general attitude toward the "Seventh Symphony" which I feel is erroneous, is the common belief that this music is supposed to contain the absolute voice of optimism. Anyone who is at all familiar with the trials and hardships which Beethoven endured during the period of the composition of this symphony, must wonder at the apparent lightheartedness of this masterpiece of gaiety. Critics have remarked about it, and it is little wonder that they have. However, without wishing to belittle the abstract beauty of the "Seventh Symphony" by placing definite labels on its emotional content, it has always seemed to me that its finale reveals more of Beethoven's inner turbulence than many have supposed. As I shall point out in my later discussion of the finale, I feel that this music is more the revelation of the happiness of one who yearns to be happy, than of one who revels in the consummation of his happiness. Will Durant may have felt this when he was led to believe that Beethoven was not so much an optimist, as one who wanted to believe he was one.[3]

All this, of course, is only a matter of opinion, and a single movement of a symphony is surely not ample means on which to determine Beethoven's breadth of nature. Be the matter as it may, it is best to listen to the "Seventh Symphony" for the mere sake of listening to it, without judging its possible psychological revelations. This, however, is more quickly said than done. It is difficult to limit one's own reactions toward art, without committing the folly of trying to limit the reactions of others.

First Movement: Poco sostenuto; vivace

The first movement opens with a long introduction which might well have been expanded into a movement by itself. It has a distinctly pastoral flavor, for Beethoven is never quite the lovable poet unless he sings of the woods. There is a sunny cheerfulness in this introduction, utterly unlike the long introduction in the "Fourth Symphony." With masterly good humor Beethoven runs into the main theme of the vivace. There is a light-hearted gaiety in this that is full of the joy of living, and Beethoven seems like a young colt that is let loose to bound over the hills and meadows. He bounds this way and that, always full of rhythmic vitality. As he reaches the passage for horns and wind instruments he seems to swing us fully off our feet. The coda is crowded with delicious fooleries. This is music that cannot be described; one must only drink it in to one's heart's content, for it is as intoxicating as good wine. We shall see more of this in the finale.

Second Movement: Allegretto

This movement is one of the chief reasons for the popularity of the "Seventh Symphony." However, should we look for something reminiscent of the glorious tones of the slow movements of the "Third" or "Fifth" symphonies, we will end by being extremely disappointed. For this movement is not heavenly in any sense of the term; it rather has a plaintive loveliness somewhat like Schubert's exquisite variations on "Death and the Maiden." There is a clouded beauty in it, which, however, is far from mysticism. It seems like a procession of monks through the shadowy aisles of a monastery, when the departing sun softly illuminates the stained windows and casts panels of mellow light across the altar. The terrifying chord on the woodwind, which opens the movement, creates the erroneous impression that Beethoven is preparing us for a movement of the utmost austerity; but we end by feeling the music was comforting rather than forbidding. There is a delightful melodiousness in it which exercises a particular fascination over children; and at times it approaches lulling mildness. The second theme, which Beethoven introduces so beautifully, but which leaves with characteristic abruptness, forms a most tender contrast with what has gone before. The marching rhythm becomes more marked in the fugato, which is one of the outstanding portions in the entire movement. Of special interest is the subtlety of the closing portion, where the last fragments of the main theme are brought back to us, and then dissolved into nothingness. The chord on the woodwind is heard again, this time concluding the movement; but we have drunk in too much beauty to be frightened at this late time, and we are left tranquil and unruffled.

Third Movement: Scherzo e trio

The vivacity of the first movement returns, and the young colt begins bounding anew. After the procession-like serenity of the second movement, the rapidity of the third is as refreshing as a summer's shower. Those who really know Beethoven regard his moments of serenity with great distrust; not distrust of his emotional sincerity, but of his next move. That is one of his most amiable characteristics. No greater contrast has ever been offered in art than that between the second and third movements of the "Eroica"; the one in the "Seventh Symphony" is not so striking in comparison. We are to encounter such a breathless contrast again in the "Ninth Symphony," when, on the very heels of the tumultuous scherzo, Beethoven leads us directly into the divine adagio.

Once more the scent of the country returns. The opening theme is like that busy movement of life which one is wont to observe on a fine summer's morning. The woods teem with these living organisms; everything rises with the sun, and follows its own course once more. The elegiac beauty of the second movement is already like a dream of the night before, when, having beheld the night in all her purple mysteriousness, one's spirit seemed to have faded away over the silent meadows with the last broken notes of the allegretto. The horn calls are ushered in; and still again we encounter Beethoven's love for his fellow-men. Beethoven seems to throw his arms wide apart and embrace us all one by one, much in the same manner as he stood at the doorway of the Court Theatre on the memorable occasion of the first performance of the "Ninth Symphony" and embraced the musical amateurs. There is a strong rustic feeling in this trio, and at the same time a colorful glow of healthy romanticism. This movement does not follow the conventional form of the minuet, in which the trio is sandwiched between the first appearance and the concluding repetition of the main theme. This movement is rather like a series of sandwiches, in which the scherzo and trio follow one another in steady order. It was in the scherzo of the "Sixth Symphony" that we first encountered such repetitions, but in the "Seventh" the form is broadened generously, and the return of the themes are a constant delight. Beethoven becomes his most characteristic self at the very end, when, beginning the trio with suspicious slowness, he cuts it short abruptly with five decisive chords. "I think it's about enough," he seems to say. "I must take a little nap before the finale." Let us see what happens when he awakes.

Finale: Allegro con brio

From this movement, more than from any other, one can find Beethoven's justification for his words to Bettina Brentano: "*Moi je suis Bacchus qui pressure pour les hommes le nectar délicieux*" (I am the Bacchus who presses out the delicious wine for men). According to the questionable testimony of Bettina, he is also supposed to have added the phrase, "which intoxicates their souls." And here indeed is this intoxication. This music is possessed of a wild and Bacchanalian frenzy; it is a Herculean unloosening of all man's pent-up emotions. Such super-abundance of energy is inconceivable in a single man. It is like the wild revelry of the drunken gods of Olympus. One can well understand how even a genius like Weber, who composed the epoch-making "Freischütz" staggered beneath the breathless sweep of those impetuous rhythms and declared hopelessly, "Beethoven is on his way to the mad-house." For Weber had never conceived of such titanic orgies in music; it confused him, and caused him to doubt his own senses. This music symbolizes one of those very forces of Beethoven's nature from which Goethe turned aside for fear of losing his dignity. After listening to it, we can fully understand why Beethoven used to burst into fits of rage and send things flying all about him. This man's energy was so colossal that it had to come out, even as rocks fly from a volcano. Who can say if this does not reveal the flooding wells of Beethoven's sexual nature, which, repressed for a great length of time, came rushing forth in this superhuman outlet? But it is not one emotion alone which is released; it is all emotions released together, with one grand, fearless gesture. Every now and then we can catch a trace of boisterousness which is essentially Russian in character. Beethoven never quite loses his taste for Russian melodies: we find this fondness for them asserting itself again in the Rasoumowsky quartets, as well as in the finale of the "Eroica" and in the scherzo of the "Pastoral." There is something of the Russian abandonment to revelry in his own turbulent nature. Despite all the spontaneous merriment of this finale, however, I do not feel convinced that it is an absolute expression of optimism. It seems as though Beethoven were so obsessed with his real or imaginary woes that he felt the overwhelming desire to free himself from them entirely. This must have been the case with Mozart when, oppressed by financial difficulties as well as by ill health, he threw himself headlong into the restless surge of the finale of the "G minor symphony." The outcome of such extreme assertion of self-will is often an unbalancing of man's inner harmony. The man who found himself at the brink of despair a short time ago, becomes the new creature who, for all his reckless abandonment to joy, is an even more pitiful spectacle than before. In his desire to drown his sorrows, he laughs, shouts, cries, dances, and whirls himself round and round as though bitten by the tarantula. Finally he falls to the ground, and weary in body and soul he dozes off. On awaking, he finds himself the man he knew himself to be previously; and, save for his dizziness, which still lingers in his brain and which recalls his orgies to his mind, his wild outbursts are already like a dream out the distant past. This is probably what Beethoven must have felt after he had written the last note of this finale. But who can say whether if this really was the case, Beethoven did not find that his past revels had been well worthwhile? At any rate, they are a glorious heritage to us, for they teach us how to laugh with a man who all too often laughed through tears.

THE EIGHTH SYMPHONY IN F MAJOR, OPUS 93 "THE LITTLE SYMPHONY"

First Movement: Allegro vivace e con brio

This is Beethoven's little package of drolleries; his little earthly holiday before he ascends to the vast sublimities of the "Ninth Symphony."

The first movement opens without the slightest introduction. This at once prepares us for the utter directness which is to follow. Here there is no profound thought, no titanic conflicts, no ethereal melancholy. There is spontaneity throughout, every phrase moving forward straight to the point. In the realm of the drama it is comparable to the breezy hastiness of Ibsen's "Enemy of the People." We are reminded of Beethoven's letters to his friends, crowded full of lovable childishness. Here and there are jerky rhythms; energetic chords, like frogs leaping in a sun-lit pool; sudden pauses and amiable repetitions; and gnome-like pranks. No music more reveals that side of Beethoven's nature which never aged, and which remained genial and sunny until the end. For this is music which no misanthrope could have written. It is the first and last words in pure, unaffected optimism. It is not like the stupendous optimism of the "Fifth Symphony," but optimism of healthy, earthly origin, which the common, as well as the great can fully experience. This universality is Beethoven's greatest gift.

Second Movement: Allegretto scherzando

Let us reflect that the self-same man who had composed the sublimities of the "Eroica" and "Fifth" symphonies, and who was yet to journey forth late into the supreme regions of the intellect in the "Ninth Symphony,"—let us reflect that this very man composed this childishly simple allegretto. This music is a little masterpiece of droll, impish humor. It is like Beethoven himself telling an amusing little tale to a group of friends in a tavern. The theme is built against the continual tick-tock of Mälzel's chronometer, which is initiated in the woodwind instruments. From this lovable simplicity Mendelssohn's fairy music eventually originated.[4] Beethoven appears in his truest self when he tires of his fooleries and brings the movement to an abrupt conclusion with a smack of Italian-like flavor, which was probably intended as a caricature of Rossini. We must love with all our hearts a man who could indulge in such delicious fancies. "Haydn has never really died," we may declare on hearing this music; "the Prince of Gaiety lives again; and the ever-youthful soul of Beethoven is his dwelling-place.[5]"

Third Movement: Tempo di minuetto

This is the only movement in all of Beethoven's symphonies that is written in the true tempo of the minuet; and it is precisely this which has caused some people to suppose that Beethoven is returning to his first period. Nothing could be more erroneous. True, it savors of Mozart, but the main theme contains a summery breeziness which is Beethoven's very own. There is a pleasing swing and vitality throughout, and one can feel that Beethoven is in his best spirits. The middle section is one of exquisite rural beauty, which still again recalls those earlier tries which seemed to speak of universal brotherhood. In few places does Beethoven fill us with such sheer delight and charmed feelings of unadorned simplicity. As we are swung back into the main theme again, we are happy indeed that Beethoven has, for the last time, revived those gentle whisperings of his predecessors. He has brought Mozart to life, but has given him a pinch of salt from his own personality. It is his last tribute to one of his spiritual fathers.

Fourth Movement: Allegro vivace

Beethoven returns to his very own speech, and a boisterous speech it is. The opening theme, with its wild surrender to rollicking fun, reveals Beethoven in one of his most "unbuttoned" moods. There is simply no holding him back; his movements are like those of a domestic animal in which the savage blood of its forefathers is awakened. From wild joy he mounts to Bacchanalian revelry, and does not pause even at the boundary of brutal coarseness. Yet if he is coarse, he has never been so more fittingly. It is his final outburst of untamed hilarity before he enters, like a high priest, into the solemn regions of the "Ninth Symphony" and the "Missa Solemnis." But the second theme! Never was there a more extreme contrast between a first and second melody in a symphonic movement. From his exuberant overflowing of spirits he leads us directly into a theme of the utmost gentleness and serenity. It is as though a drunkard had paused amid his reckless bursts of movement and but dimly recalled a beautiful image of the past. It is to forget this image that he had drunk of the intoxicating flask; and now it returns, like a dim shadow out of his inner consciousness. Is it the shadow of Beethoven's own frustrated love-life which comes to haunt him when he desires most to forget it? Is it the phantom of the capricious face of Giulietta Guicciardi? or perhaps that of the stately and learned Therese von Brunswick? or still perhaps that of his Hungarian idolatress, the Countess Erdődy, his "*liebe, liebe, liebe, liebe Gräfin*" (dear, dear, dear, dear Countess — [ed. trans.])? As Villon has said,

> *Mais où sont les neiges d'antan?*
> (But where are the snows of yesteryear? — [ed. trans.])

Beethoven has acquired that sad philosophy which tells him that our wildest moments of joy are overcast with shadows of repressed longings. He spoke of it in the finale of the "Fifth Symphony," when, said his triumphant paeans of joy, a sombre cloud of the past reappeared, only to give way once more to the final outburst of jubilation. Even so is this fitful vision of melancholy dispelled in the "Little Symphony"; it is drowned in the whirlpool of joy, and Beethoven continues to whirl round and round until he drops with sweet exhaustion. Now he shall rest, while the majestic heavens breathe forth the glories of his last symphonic achievement.

THE NINTH SYMPHONY IN D MINOR, OPUS 125; WITH A FINAL CHORUS ON SCHILLER'S "ODE TO JOY"

First Movement: Allegro ma non troppo un poco maestoso

Had Beethoven written nothing more but the colossal first movement of the "Ninth Symphony," he would still have been great enough to join hands with Michelangelo. This music is the most complete musical equivalent of "The Creation" as depicted in Michelangelo's Sistine frescos. Nowhere in the entire realm of instrumental music is there anything more stupendous and giant-like than the towering opening of this symphony. The mysterious quality of the unique introduction is like the reigning darkness of chaos, or like the quiet sinking of the soul into oblivion. Out of chaos a streak of lightning seems to appear, piercing the dark corners of the earth. The streak is widened into an oblique panel of light, and the heavenly portals are thrown wide open as thunder breaks over our heads. In an instant the light is caught, subdued, and hurled back into oblivion whence it came. This feat is not one of a mere musician, but of a giant possessed of the strength of Atlas. One recalls Beethoven's words, "I always have some picture in mind when I am composing, and on that I work." These words now fill one with awe, if not with terror. What, then, was the precise picture in Beethoven's mind when he composed the opening of this symphony? The question is as disturbing as the recollection of some terrible nightmare evoked by ghastly phantoms out of opium dreams. We say, "Away with this question! It is meaningless"; but it clings to us like the horror of death itself.

Chaos reigns again. As once again the spark of brightness is expanded into a panel of flooding light, the thought now occurs to us: "Does this represent Beethoven himself emerging from darkness into light?" What represents darkness and light for Beethoven? Is it outer deafness merged into an inner symphony of sound? No one can say. Beethoven himself once wrote (and these words, taken from an Egyptian tomb, were his life-long motto), "I am he who exists. I

53

am all that is, that was, and shall be. No mortal man has lifted my veil. He is one only. Self-created, and to that Only One all things owe their being." "No mortal man has lifted my veil"! And indeed, it is to be wondered whether anyone has. At first this seems like colossal self-confidence precipitating the mind into gulfs of madness; but on closer examination one is startled by the true meaning of these words. While Beethoven knew that he was not the present, past, and future, he justly felt that his genius was symbolic of all three. The opening of the "Ninth Symphony" is in itself broad enough for the justification of such a self-opinion; it is no less a phenomenon of Nature than his very genius itself. To attempt to analyze it is to stagger at the prodigious attempt. One must accept it as it penetrates the ear and the inner soul, merely as one of the unfathomable mysteries of Beethoven's creative mind.

This time, when Beethoven subdues the light he has created, he casts it away with rugged fury. Out of this emerges a new theme, tender and poignant, like the second theme of the first movement of the "Fifth Symphony," or like the theme of womanly influence in the "Coriolanus Overture." The first theme, as compared with the second, is like one of Beethoven's tempestuous rages against the suspicious actions of the universe, melting into a sudden appearance of over-tender emotions toward his nephew, Carl. These varied emotions are as eternally present in him as in the contrasting tones of Nature.

Let us observe the peculiar rhythm of this music as we are led up to the coda. It is unlike that of any other movement in all of the other symphonies. Its flow is like the gradual movement of lava flowing down the sides of a volcano. Everything lies buried under the eruption, and the atmosphere is crowded with imaginary voices of despair crying out from the slimy depths. Occasionally the theme of tenderness reappears, only to be followed by still more impassioned outbursts. Once again the heavens are rent asunder, and shafts of light strike obliquely at the rolling masses below. As we enter the coda, we know that the new world is nearing its completion. Towers crumble and hurl their rocks down to earth, reminding us of Poe's House of Usher falling into the waves. Those terrible words describing the awful spectacle bear peculiar resemblance to the picture evoked by the coda:—

From that chamber and from that mansion I fled aghast. The storm was still abroad in all its wrath as I found myself crossing the old causeway. Suddenly there shot through the path a wild light, and I turned to see whence a gleam so unusual could have issued, for the vast house and its shadows were alone behind me. The radiance was that of the full, setting, and blood-red moon, which now shone vividly through that once barely discernible fissure, of which I have before spoken as extending from the roof of the building in a zig-zag direction to the base. While I gazed, this fissure rapidly widened; there came a fierce breath of the whirlwind; the entire orb of the satellite burst at once upon my sight; my brain reeled as I saw the mighty walls rushing asunder; there was a long tumultuous shouting sound, like the voice of a thousand waters, and the deep and dark tarn at my feet closed sullenly and silently over the fragments of the House of Usher.

As the movement ends with the gigantic return of the beginning section, we know two things: firstly, that we have listened to a coda hitherto unknown in all symphonic music; and secondly, that Beethoven, like Rembrandt in his incomparable "Syndics," has at last achieved the utmost sense of inner harmony of which mortal man is capable.

The liberator stands liberated, while the civilized world looks on in awe.

On the appearance of the scherzo before the adagio

Contrary to his usual custom, Beethoven has a scherzo as his second movement, and an adagio as his third. We first received a hint of this in the "Eighth Symphony," where, however, a slow movement is omitted altogether. Let us not believe that Beethoven does this in the "Ninth Symphony" merely to prepare us for the revolutionary choral finale. Beethoven is subtle in this, as in all things pertaining to his art; and his genius has always been responsive only to the highest in his domain. He must have felt intuitively that the adagio was more fitting as a third movement, directly before the joyous ascension of the soul in the finale. Beethoven's meaning was probably that the soul is first fully purified before it gains admittance into the realms of true happiness. This was the philosophy with which Beethoven lived, and which brought him to his ultimate triumph both as a man and as an artist. Nowhere is this process of purification better expressed than in the slow movement of this symphony: truly it is Beethoven's realm of heavenly ideals. More than that; it is the orchestral equivalent of the passage in Handel's "Messiah" which is sung to the following words: "And he shall purify the sons of Levi." The purification which Handel depicts, however, is one originating from a single source and involving a mere group; the source being the influence of Jesus, and the group, "the sons of Levi." With Beethoven it is not so. The adagio oversteps all the boundaries of religion, and takes on an aspect of the most universal beauty. We shall hear more about this breadth and sublimity in the section devoted exclusively to the third movement of the symphony.

Second Movement: Scherzo; molto vivace

Just as the first movement of the "Ninth Symphony" stands alone among all the introductory movements of Beethoven's nine symphonies, so does the scherzo of this same symphony tower above all previous ones. Rossini marveled at it, and with good cause. Although he was only "a peddler of melodies," as Beethoven called him, he recognized supreme greatness when he encountered it. "But that scherzo, that scherzo!" the Swan of Pesaro is supposed to have remarked on first hearing the symphony. Such a superabundance of energy is not present even in the finale of the "Seventh Symphony." It dwarfs all scherzos of the later romanticists. Indeed, it is almost as though Beethoven had decided, once and for all, to let all his energy run loose and overflow its own walls of resistance. The result is an outburst of tumultuous power which seems like the moving of a thousand giants engines, each moving by an individual process of locomotion apart from the others. Could Vesuvius acquire ears, she would undoubtedly have asked what mortal man had dared assail her own powers in this fashion. The very opening of this stupendous scherzo is like the fall of a giant hammer on our heads. Then the steady movement begins, like the continuous noises of all earthly beings joining in one deafening symphony. There is a pause, as though all the forces of life had stopped to gather new energy. Once again the Russian flavor appears amid Beethoven's delirium of action. But this is not enough; he calls the kettledrum to his aid, and amuses himself with them as though they were toys. Onward, onward this wheel of life turns. The sledge-hammer falls; we reel with dizziness; too much—too much—we can bear no more. Now we may sleep,—the everlasting slumber of the weary. But though we sleep, action still continues. It goes on within us, in our dreams, when the engines begin their locomotion from the very beginning; and it continues from without, from the very rotation of the earth down to the tiny creatures that fly around flickering night lamp. It is life—and we are part of the great, immeasurable whole.

Third Movement: Adagio molto e cantabile

This is the beginning of Wagner's mysticism. This music overflows with a beauty never surpassed in any of Beethoven's other adagios, and that is the beauty of divine purity. It awakens feelings akin to those one experiences when gazing at the rapt face of Raphael's "Madonna del Granduca"; and yet one finds such beauty even more evident in the bittersweet smiles of the heavenly women of Leonardo da Vinci. For this music is not like a mere smile of purity; it is rather like the smile of purity attained by suffering. Hence such heavenly poetry is not to be found in the face of the Madonna who adores her Child; it is to be found rather in the face of the Madonna who has already witnessed the Crucifixion. Herein is the philosophy of Beethoven's own existence. Suffering ennobles the commonplace man, and makes the great even greater. It is with inner pain that we realize that such sublime beauty was reserved for Beethoven's last symphony; a fact which itself is symbolic of the truth that the highest perfection in life and art is reached only after all but the last effort has been exhausted. It is as though it was always Man's last achievement that comes closest to the divine. The presence of death, which already breathes its cold breath on man, fills the mortal with a frantic desire to prove that he is submitting to the outer forces with the grandeur of one who is their equal. Hence he acquires new wisdom, new depth of utterance, and a sense of beauty which pains one by its very celestial qualities. Such was the case with Mozart when he soared heavenward in his "Jupiter Symphony," the last of his symphonic masterpieces. It was also the case with Schubert when he acquired new strength of expression and till then unrealized virility in his "C major symphony," but who was snatched from life even as he stood at the very threshold of his newly-found world of Beethovenish heroism. And lastly, it was no different with Beethoven who, as the adagio of the "Ninth Symphony" neared its completion, was separated from the grave by only four or five years.

How can one begin the brutal task of analyzing such abstract beauty? How can one conceive of such music flowing from more instruments? The opening theme is full of such serene and blissful poetry that one is pained to hear such music pass away. This theme is in itself a proof of Beethoven's inner nobility, for only one of the highest spiritual dignity could have conceived it. It is like the meeting of heaven and earth, while all living creatures look on in wonder and swell with the sheer beauty of living. Even the short introduction to this principle theme glows with ethereal light and majesty. The variations cannot be described: words must fail when they attempt to overstep their concrete boundaries. The second theme is one of the most exquisite and haunting melancholy. For a while Beethoven acquires that gentle persuasiveness of Schubert; and yet it seems more like an anticipation of the brooding lyricism of Tchaikovsky. Beethoven caresses his themes as though they were the breath of life to him; they are his favorite children, and he is loath to tear them from his heart. He interweaves them; now in a chance of rhythm, now in a change of key; but the same tone of exalted beauty is maintained throughout. Suddenly we are startled by what appears like a blast from heaven. There is a prophetic grandeur in this, as though Beethoven, like Moses, were receiving the Ten Commandments on Mount Sinai. The passage which follows between this and the second blast is like an angelic plea for the heavenly benediction on all mankind. The creatures of the earth seem to turn their eyes upward in a mute entreaty for everlasting peace. Peace! When will it come? and whence? Silence. It comes...but not yet...not yet...

Last Movement: Choral finale

A commotion; the earth is upheaved. Silence again. A question floats upward on the cellos, like the Hebrews crying by the waters of Babylon. Where is this peace which we have been promised? We do not see it. Is it in the air? perchance in the heavens? ... Silence! The earth is shaken again, and its bowels rent asunder. The time is not yet at hand. Darkness again. Chaos. Out of this comes the first breath of joy; joy on wings of anticipation. The opening themes of the previous movements are reviewed in swift succession. Yes, joy cometh! Does it come from chaos? from the vigorous movement of the desire to regain life? or from the re-purification of the soul? It matters not. It cometh, and by itself ... independent of the outer forces! The Theme of Joy ... sublime, descending joy ... is ushered in; ... but not at once. For joy cometh slowly, like a faint light breaking in on the vision with growing intensity. We beckon it nearer, and it cometh slowly. It is the will ... the inconquerable will which draws it nearer to us. It is now upon us fully, and we stand bathed in light. Are we masters of the light, or is the light master of us? Neither. We are one ... united in joy! Then away with all selfish desires! "O brothers, not these tones!" sings the baritone voice (*O Freunde, nicht diese Tone!*); and all stand united and listening. To the accompaniment of sweeping chords, the men cry out, "Ye millions, embrace one another!" (*Seid umschlungen, Millionen!*) It is the cry of the deaf Beethoven to all humanity. The women join in, for they too have been freed. Isolated voices, the cries of the individual, are heard; but they are drowned out by the appearance of the masses, for joy can exist only in unity. Such is the thought with which the finale concludes. Beethoven comes out of himself, and embraces the world.

On the worth of the choral finale

The greatest error of Beethoven's life lies in the very composition of the choral finale. He had conceived it when he was barely twenty, and executed it in his fifties. Had he lived a few years longer, he might have rectified the error by omitting the chorus completely and replacing it by an orchestral finale. Beethoven was chiefly an artist of the highest abstract order, and so should he have remained. The orchestral beginning of the finale of the "Ninth Symphony" is wonderful for the sole reason that Beethoven does not overstep his own domains. The instrumental recitative is of a highly inspired order. Even the voices at the beginning have grandeur, and the entrance of the baritone voice is truly sublime. But what happens later? To the untrained ear Beethoven becomes strange and discordant. To pretend that one feels the highest sublimity in all of these choral passages is to do injustice to those of Beethoven's works which are truly sublime. Seldom does the chorus rise to those heavenly heights of Handel which seem to carry the soul upward amid flames. Rarely do we find passages to compare with the breathless rapture of the Hallelujah Chorus from Handel's "Messiah," or with the vibrant "Thanks be to God" from Mendelssohn's "Elijah." As soon as the orchestra reappears, Beethoven reappears with it. The incomparable theme of joy, which Brahms was later to recapture in the finale of his "First Symphony," and with which Schubert was to introduce the new Beethovenish spirit in the finale of his "C major symphony," is glorious ... but only while Beethoven alters it in the orchestra. When the chorus takes it up, they often reduce it to a pitiful imitation of inspired feeling. Beethoven's words to Wegeler fully explain the deficiencies of this whole choral finale. "I often compose the answer (i.e., to a letter) in my head, but when I wish to write it down I gradually throw aside my pen, from not being able to write as I feel." This is what happened to Beethoven when he passed from the abstract to the concrete. And let us remember that Beethoven wrote these words three years after the composition of the "Ninth Symphony," which is sufficient evidence of the fact that he must have been aware of his shortcomings a long time previously.[6] This, then ... the very task of setting words to music ... was the greatest error of the self-same man who had once said to Bettina Brentano some years before the composition of the "Ninth Symphony," "My kingdom is in the air (*Mein Reich ist in der luft*)." This is the sole reason why the choral finale of Beethoven's greatest symphonic masterpiece, while a gigantic attempt, is only a futile execution.[7]

A FINAL CONSIDERATION OF BEETHOVEN AND HIS ACHIEVEMENTS

Beethoven has been called the Shakespeare of music. He is much more than that. If poetic England has her Shakespeare, she also has her Milton; Germany has her Goethe; Italy, her Dante; Russia, her Pushkin. By universal consent all these men must yet pay homage to Homer as the greatest poet of of them all. Neither is Shakespeare supreme as a dramatist. In our own age Ibsen, far removed from the Elizabethan (no less than from the Victorian) superficialities, went far beyond Shakespeare's psychological and technical achievements, while still retaining his native morbid tendencies. However one may differ on this point, it is well to remember that dramatically Shakespeare was purely a product of his times: he differed from Ibsen, as well as from Beethoven, chiefly insofar as he did not overstep the technical resources of his era.

Beethoven's position in the world of music, like that of Newton in physics, is unique; and his position among the world's greatest artists has never been surpassed. He owes his artistic origin to Bach, but he stands apart from him—a monarch of his own domains. He was one of the few supreme creators of time immemorial, and his fifty-seven years on this earth were one of the rarest gifts nature ever bestowed on mankind.

I have said that Beethoven's position in the world of music is unique; but, as I have already said elsewhere, it was so while he remained an instrumentalist. It is well that it was so. Had nature endowed him with Schubert's lyric spontaneity, he might, like him, have been a nightingale rather than an eagle. Neither was he possessed of Mozart's amazing spirit of productiveness; the essential difference between the two lies in the fact that Mozart was born into music, whereas Beethoven had to force his way into it through pillars of stone. He possessed none of Wagner's genius necessary for supreme creations for the stage, nor Handel's genius for religious masterpieces. In short, he was Beethoven and only Beethoven. As a symphonist of the romantic era, only Schubert and Brahms can compare with him. He was their model, their spiritual father. His influence sounds from Brahms's mightiest symphonies down to the delicate elfin music of Mendelssohn. His chamber music is a priceless glory to art—the most intimate diary of his truly noble soul. Even his concerti, with their occasional displays of virtuosity, are stamped with the highest and most eternal utterances of genius. His works must remain a deathless beauty, an everlasting consolation to the human heart. He not only emancipated the instrumental forms of music, but liberated the soul from its petty bonds of convention, and brought light to the clouded vision of humanity. His life and work are a prophecy of the fullest beauty and nobility—a prophecy of what Beethoven himself might have referred to as "that ever distant goal" toward which the world continues to move, but which it can but dimly see through curtains of mist. To those who strive he is like a distant sun, forever beckoning them onward. He is their teacher, their comforter, and their confessor. He was imperfect as a man, even as Phidias must have been; but he had enough essential goodness of heart to improvise on the pianoforte for a mother who had lost her child. "Now I shall speak to you through tones," he said to her,—he who, on previous occasions, had to be drawn to the pianoforte by friends' cleverly invented stratagems. And he seated himself at the keyboard and played until she was comforted. And as she sat lost in reveries, he arose quietly and departed. Even so has he communed with the world, and left it with little ceremony. He is gone, but he is with us for, as Shelly has so divinely said of Keats,

> The soul of Adonais, like a star,
> Beacons from the abode where the eternal are.

NOTES

1. (page 36) Programme music dates much further back than the period of Beethoven. It is even to be found in Bach; but in the "Pastoral Symphony" it was broadened beyond the means of Beethoven's predecessors.

2. (page 44) Of course, this does not include the first and second symphonies.

3. (page 45) See "The Story of Philosophy" for Will Durant's comment on Beethoven's optimism.

4. (page 51) It is also possible that Mendelssohn found great inspiration in the elfin music of Weber; notably in the overture to "Oberon."

5. (page 51) It is worthwhile to observe that Haydn also once indulged in such humor—namely, in the second movement of the "Clock Symphony."

6. (page 60) "Fidelio," Beethoven's only opera, had proved a dismal failure as far back as 1804, and at present is performed very rarely...As far as I am aware, his oratorio, "The Mount of Olives," has not, in recent years, been once revived in the churches of New York. In my opinion, his only two great choral works are his "Missa Solemnis" and "Praise of God in Nature."

7. (page 60) One may well say that Schubert, in the finale of his "C major symphony," more closely approached the highest Beethovenish ideals than Beethoven himself did in the choral finale of his "Ninth Symphony."

AFTERWORD

I will be forever grateful for the day my dear friend Mike Bengis approached me holding a faded manuscript. "Hey! I know you like classical music—I think you'll get a kick out of this."

As I read, I became dizzy with excitement. In my hands was a record of urgency, written in an ecstatic frenzy by a young man who lived long ago in a time before the modern distractions of television and the internet. Mike's uncle, Jerome Bengis, writes of being enthralled by the great music of Beethoven. The centuries melted away as I read Jerome's reactions to the nine symphonies, which he describes movement by movement.

Such passion! This manuscript reveals where Jerome's heart lies, and he declares his highest praise for the creativity and genius of the composer who lived more than a century earlier.

However, as Jerome listens to the fevered finale, he voices a note of confused disappointment. He decries Beethoven's choice to end the Ninth, this last and greatest symphony, with a choral accompaniment to the orchestra. How could the musical master not know that the human voice could not be expected to keep pace with the fervor which could be produced by instrumentalists?

Beethoven began his career in classical music at the height of the period when the brilliance of Mozart and other musicians had already and undeniably perfected the art of bringing sound to fruition. Jerome details in his explication how Beethoven goes on to expand even further the expressive possibilities for music. He revels in sharing his appreciation for the joy this discovery brings him.

It is evidence of Beethoven's genius that his final symphony contains innovations, not only in how man can create an experience in sound, but also in how man can experience what it means to be human. The Ninth brings to individual people a personal awareness of the dawning of a new era in human history.

Even today we are swept away by the conclusion, when we come to understand the significance offered by the lyrics. As the orchestra soars to new heights, the choir sings the words "brotherhood" and "joy"—and it is the listener's emotional reaction, on comprehending his own connection with this wonder of human existence, which completes the performance. We become one with the music, with the orchestra, and with all of humanity: united, a perfect brotherhood of man.

How incredible it must have been, to be there in person, as "Ode to Joy" filled the hall for the first time. The great composer, though deaf, had created the most magnificent of all musical masterpieces and, at the same time, linked us with one another, heart to heart.

Standing on stage facing the orchestra, Beethoven could not hear a thing. He lowered his baton in utter silence—and had to be prompted by a tap on the shoulder to turn around and face his audience . . .

. . . and he saw the great horde leaping from their seats into the aisles, wildly clapping and cheering, rushing the stage in ecstasy over his magnificent gift!

Susanna Lee

ABOUT THE AUTHOR

Jerome Bengis, 89, a life long resident of the Bronx, died in 2002 on May 28th at Newton Memorial Hospital, NJ. He is remembered as a gentle person with a ribald, almost juvenile sense of humor and a bottomless knowledge and love of classical music. He was the author of 13 plays, including several written just for children.

As a young man he boldly sent enthusiastic notes to those in the arts he admired, and often received replies, with an opportunity to meet such idols. Once, reveling in the company of an operatic singer, he casually tossed down a martini, then bolted from the room choking, with an olive lodged in his throat.

In 1949, his play *The Silent Years*, dramatizing the period of Jesus' life not illuminated by scripture, was performed at Converse College, Spartenburg, SC. Mr. Bengis was an ever interested and keen observer of life, and took unfailing delight in his surroundings. He would have agreed that NYC held all he needed. South Carolina was the farthest afield he ever went, but his perceptions extended far beyond that locale.

One of six children, Jerome Bengis was born in 1913 to Russian/Lithuanian parents. Burdened with familial duties, he never finished high school, but soon confirmed his commitment to music when at age 24 he authored a critical monograph, *Beethoven and his Nine Symphonies*. Oberlin College favorably acknowledged this work.

He and his late wife Isabelle, who died in 1998, lived in the Pelham Bay section of NYC. They had no children.

Michael Bengis

ABOUT THE COVER

The portrait of Beethoven depicted on the cover had been a gift to the Bengis family by the artist, whose name has since been forgotten, but who had drawn inspiration from the family's love of the great composer. It hung in the family's home during the life of the author and was found in the attic during the sale of his estate, along with the book's manuscript.

Michael Bengis

Published by Rose Mason Press

Cubist Poetry Series: 6 volumes

by Susanna Lee

Great Blue Heron: Haiku
Twisted Carrot: Petite Poems
My Husband's Roses: One-Page Poems
God Laughs: Longer Poems
Snow Balls: Short Stories
Fluffy Muffins: Recipes for My Peeps

Genius in 9 Symphonies: How Beethoven Reinvented Music

by Jerome Bengis

Sunrise Mountain: Haiku and Other Poetry

by Susanna Lee

Made in the USA
Middletown, DE
20 September 2022

73499856R00046